HOW TO PROTECT YOUR CREATIVITY

By Ade Asefeso MCIPS MBA

TABLE OF CONTENTS

This publication is designed to provide competent and reliable information regarding the subject matter covered. However, it is sold with the understanding that the author and publisher are not engaged in rendering professional advice. The authors and publishers specifically disclaim any liability that is incurred from the use or application of contents of this book.

If you purchased this book without a cover you should be aware that this book may have been stolen property and reported as "unsold and destroyed" to the publisher. In this case neither the author nor the publisher has received any payment for this "stripped book."

Visit our website http://www.aaglobalsourcing.com

Chapter 1: Introduction

People seem to have the misconception that only a select few are able to unleash a steady flow of creative genius. That is not true at all. The fact is, creativity is very much like a muscle that needs to be exercised in order to consistently give out great results. If you don't practice harnessing creative thinking, this skill will very much atrophy into inexistence. But keep working and this skill will soon come to you in a snap.

So how do you unleash your creative thinking? Well, the first thing is to become a human leech. No, I am not talking about just sucking the blood out of every living being available, I am saying that you should take in as much knowledge and learning you can find. Read everything available; good and bad, and keep your mind open to the infinite possibilities of the universe. The more you know, the more you will want to know, and the more your faculty of wonder will be exercised. Prepare to be amazed at little facts that add a bit of colour into your life.

Focus on a creative activity everyday. Yes, it's an effort. Even doodling is a creative activity. Don't let anything hinder you. Mindlessness may be a creative activity, but for people who are just starting out to unleash a little bit of creative thinking in their lives, it is helpful and encouraging to have concrete evidence, that, "hey, what I'm doing is getting somewhere." So why don't you try it. Practice drawing for a couple of minutes each day. Bring out your old camera and start snapping photos like crazy. Keep a journal and make a point to write in it religiously. Another cool idea is to write by describing something with your five senses. Try to avoid vague adjectives like "marvelous," "amazing," and "delicious." Before you know it, you will have built yourself a tiny portfolio, and you will be amazed at the growth you have undertaken after amassing all those works of art. Who knows, you might actually take to liking those things you do everyday. Pretty soon those things will become a part of you and you will be addicted to these creative exercises.

Think out of the box or don't. Sometimes, constraints are actually a good thing. Limitations discipline you to work within your means. It enables you to be more resourceful. Creative freedom is great, but limitations enforce discipline.

Try something new everyday and let your experiences broaden your perspective. Explore a new district in your neighborhood. Spend an afternoon in a museum to which you have never been before. Chat up someone on the bus. Open up to the people around you. As you thrust yourself out of your comfort zone more and more each day, your sense of adventure grows and so does your zest for life.

Think about it. When was the last time you did something for the first time? If it is been a while, I tell you, you have been missing out on a whole lot of experiences that could have added to your growth, emotionally, mentally, physically, or spiritually. Why don't you try bungee jumping today? Not only will you learn, but you will also have plenty of stories to share, enabling you to practice your storytelling skills and making you the life of the party.

Embrace insanity. No, not to the point of practically

admitting yourself into the mental ward. As John Russell once said, "Sanity calms, but madness is more interesting." Exactly! Every creative thought was once deemed insanity by other "normal" people at one time or another. Luckily, that didn't stop the creative geniuses from standing by them.

The thing is, sanity or being normal confines people to think... well, normally. Creativity is essentially breaking through barriers. Yes, this includes the bizarre and the downright strange. I'm not saying that you yourself should develop a creative personality. That might go haywire. An example of a creative personality would be George Washington, who often rode into battle naked, or James Joyce, who wrote "Dubliners" with beetle juice for an intense fear of ink, or Albert Einstein, who thought his cat was a spy sent by his rival (or in thinking creatively in this case, the term could probably be "archnemesis.") It's important that your creativity doesn't get you detached from the real world completely.

I hope this chapter has inspired you to start thinking beyond your "limits." If you follow these steps pretty soon you will be living a life full of interesting adventures. Unleashing your creative thinking will bring about a new zest for living life.

As soon as you start work on your creative invention, you need to be thinking of easy way to protect your invention from being copied in any form. You can do this by applying for an invention patent. Protecting the invention from any unauthorized usage is the right of every inventor. The inventor can exercise this right using an invention patent. Generally people have a habit of copying something that is invented and which is useful.

These people without taking prior permission from the inventor publish it in the books and earn lot of money. To stop these malpractices, you can take the help of invention patent. If you have an invention patent and some other person with hateful intentions is trying to copy or sell your invention without your permission then you can sue that person.

If the person is found guilty then he or she is bound to go to jail. Patent laws prevent others from using, making, importing or selling your invention; this is applicable for a limited period

If you want to give a new style, configuration, ornamental design or decorative appearance to an existing invention then you have to apply for a design patent. Design patent does not allow you to improve the function of the existing product. A design patent has a limited period of 14 years.

If you want to functionally improve an existing invention then you have to apply for a utility patent. The existing invention can be a process or a machine.

In order to get an invention patent make ensure that your patent qualifies the eligibility criteria. You will be getting a patent only if your invention is useful to mankind. It should also be inventive and new.

Although you yourself cannot use the invention even if you get the patent, you can exclude others using or selling the patented invention for a period of 14 to 20 years.

In fact an invention patent is nothing but a right that is temporary which is offered by the government. In exchange you have to share the details about your invention with the public. Once you get an invention patent you have the right to sell, mortgage, transfer or assign it to other person. This deal may fetch you enormous amount of money.

Patent laws differ slightly in some countries. Acquiring an invention patent does not mean that the owner can exploit the patent. For instance many inventions nowadays are enhancements of prior inventions which are still protected by the owner of the patent. To build an improved version of an invention you must take permission from the patent owner of that invention.

You can enforce patents through civil suits. In some territories criminal penalties are sentenced to people who break patent laws. This discourages the infringer from doing any future infringement activities. But if you apply for compensation for infringement after the time period of invention patent then you are not liable to get any compensation in the form of money.

In order to get an invention patent, you have to pay some money to the concerned patent office of that country.

Chapter 2: How To Use Creativity To Improve Your Life

"Are there still original ideas in the world?" "They beat me to that bright idea; what else can I do?" "I've failed many times before that I can't think of anything else to solve this problem anymore."

These statements reflect the thought of an individual who has given up on creativity. Sadly, a lot of people share this way of thinking. They never viewed creativity as a very useful tool to improve or improvise in life in all its diversity.

A situation that requires a solution can be approached in a variety of ways. There isn't a single way fix to a problem. Being creative opens new horizons and can deliver many benefits. Creativity can sometimes be mistakenly interpreted as an obstinate attitude. Some people think that insisting on doing things in a different way is a sign of stubbornness.

Never hold back a good idea. Everyone is free to interpret his own unique way. Any interpretation by itself is creativity at work. A person who enjoys creative thinking can easily come up with innovative solutions for situations that require a quick fix.

For instance, your car got stalled on a deserted highway due to a leaky rubber hose on the cooling system. Tough luck! Of all places, it had to happen in the remotest places.

If you have some chewing gum in your pocket, it just might be a handy fix. Start chewing the gum and patch it on the leak. To keep the gum in place, tie it with a piece of rag.

This quick fix might do the trick so you can drive several miles without an overheated engine, until you get to a service station to have the leaky hose replaced.

There used to be a television series entitled "MacGyver." The main character is an extremely creative and crafty guy. Whenever he finds himself in a tight fix, he tries to find a way out of it with his quick fixes utilizing available materials around him.

In a way, creativity is a never-ending learning process. From learning, you gain untold benefits, which you can use in real life situations.

Being creative might require you to think out-of-the-box, venturing your mind into the uncommon. You can never be sure of your ideas until you try them. As long as there is no perceived danger involved, it is always worth a try.

Inventions are products of creative minds. The field of science, in whatever branch you may touch on, is invention itself. Without creative minds, science would have been a forlorn field of knowledge.

It must be noted that most adaptations to improve or improvise are aimed at improving current conditions. Upon analyzing honest applications of creativity, the ultimate intention is to achieve good for all and the will to build lasting peace. After all, this intention is what counts most.

Erich Fromm spelled it out clearly, "The conditions for creativity are: to be puzzled, to concentrate, to accept conflict and tension, to be born everyday, and to feel a sense of self."

Chapter 3: Definitions Of A Trademark, Copyright, And Patent Overview

A trademark is a distinctive sign or indicator used by an individual, business organization, or other legal entity to identify that the products or services to consumers with which the trademark appears originate from a unique source, and to distinguish its products or services from those of other entities.

A trademark may be designated by the following symbols: ™ (for an unregistered trade mark, that is, a mark used to promote or brand goods) ℠ (for an unregistered service mark, that is, a mark used to promote or brand services) ® (for a registered trademark)

Copyright is a way of protecting both unpublished and published literary, artistic and scientific works, and any forms of expressions as long as it is tangible. It means you can touch it, hear it, or see it. An essay, a play, a song, funky original choreography, HTML coding, or graphics can be protected. Laws of copyright grant the creator's exclusive rights to distribute, display, perform, reproduce, and prepare derivative works publicly.

A patent is a set of exclusive rights granted by a state (national government) to an inventor or their assignee for a limited period of time in exchange for a public disclosure of an invention.

The procedure for granting patents, the requirements placed

on the patentee, and the extent of the exclusive rights vary widely between countries according to national laws and international agreements. Typically, however, a patent application must include one or more claims defining the invention which must be new, non-obvious, and useful or industrially applicable. In many countries, certain subject areas are excluded from patents, such as business methods and mental acts. The exclusive right granted to a patentee in most countries is the right to prevent others from making, using, selling, or distributing the patented invention without permission.

It is just a right to prevent others' use. A patent does not give the proprietor of the patent the right to use the patented invention, should it fall within the scope of an earlier patent.

Under the World Trade Organization's (WTO) Agreement on Trade-Related Aspects of Intellectual Property Rights, patents should be available in WTO member states for any inventions, in all fields of technology, and the term of protection available should be the minimum twenty years. Different types of patents may have varying patent terms (i.e., durations).

There are subjects which are not given patent protection. It includes mental processes, physical phenomena, abstract ideas, and nature laws. Take for instance; you can't patent a new plant, insect, or mineral found or discovered in the wilderness. Likewise, the law of gravity couldn't have patented by Newton and "E=mC2" by Einstein. Any discovery which shows characteristics of nature is not reserved for a single person since it is free to all. Nature laws and abstract ideas are reserved for public domain. Artistic, musical, dramatic, or literary works are entitled for copyright protection. Inventions which are offensive and not useful are deprived of a patent right.

The patent law is created to serve various purposes. It is found in the U.S. Constitution, Clause 8 of Section 8 of Article I stating the power of the Congress to support the advancement of useful arts and science by giving exclusive rights to inventors and authors on their discoveries and writings over a limited period of time. Thus, a patent system was created by the Congress to reward limited monopolies to the inventors on making, selling, and using their inventions.

The inventions can be made available to the public however retaining its right from preventing others to use, sell, or make the invention. Patents are considered public records once it is issued. The patent applications of inventors must disclose the best approach for using or making their patented invention. The patent can be considered invalid if you fail in this procedure.

It is a fact that mental processes and abstract ideas are not eligible for patented rights. However, the software based on mathematical algorithms receives patent protection because it does not belong on the patent scopes. Algorithm is considered as a natural law while mathematics is the primary working tool of science and technology. The Supreme Court in 1981 included inventions related to software in the patent protection. It is because the function of the program only incorporates the underlying principles of mathematical algorithms. Non-physical processes are utilized by the software to operate electronically using mathematical equations or algorithms for controlling the computer program outputs. Functional application of mathematical algorithms in computer programs can be patented. Using examples from electricity or physics are not patentable. However, the methods in which electricity are utilized for transmitting information is patentable.

An invention is qualified for a patent protection if it is new, non-obvious, and useful. The invention was never used in public before an application for a patent is done. The USPTO will reject a patent if the invention is used or sold in public by the inventor or anyone for over one year before filing a patent application. Similar or identical inventions disclose publicly by others in any parts of the world can be denied of patent rights. Prior art is not anymore considered novel.

In general, the patent claims contain the preamble or the introductory paragraph. It is followed by the elements recited as steps or means to perform a specific function. The elements can be narrowly interpreted by structure, name, or defined steps. The defenses of a patent to infringement include invalidity and non-infringement.

Chapter 4: Functions Of The Patent and Trademark Office

The Patent and Trademark Office is an agency of the U.S. Department of Commerce. The role of the Patent and Trademark Office is to provide patent protection for inventions and to register trademarks. It serves the interest of inventors and businesses with respect to their inventions and corporate, product, and service identifications. It also advises and assists the bureaus and offices of the Department of Commerce and other agencies of the Government in matters involving "intellectual property" such as patents, trademarks and semiconductor mask works.

Through the preservation, classification, and dissemination of patent information, the Office aids and encourages innovation and the scientific and technical advancement of the Nation.

In discharging its duties, the Patent and Trademark Office examines applications and grants patents on inventions when applicants are entitled to them; it publishes and disseminates patent information, records assignments of patents, maintains search files of U.S. and foreign patents and a search room for public use in examining issued patents and records. It supplies copies of patents and official records to the public. Similar functions are performed relating to trademarks.

The purpose of this book is to give you some general information about patents and the operations of the Patent and Trademark Office. I attempt to answer many of the questions commonly asked of the Patent and Trademark Office but I am not intended to be a comprehensive textbook on patent law or a guide for the patent lawyer.

Consequently, many details are omitted and complications have been avoided as much as possible. It is hoped that this book will be useful to inventors and prospective applicants for patents to students, and to others who may be interested in patents by giving them a brief general introduction to the subject.

Chapter 5: Searching For A Patent

Fear grips many inventors because they are always apprehensive that some people may use their invention or new concept for making profit. And in spite of hard work he or she will be a loser. To protect the rights of these individuals the concept of patent came into force.

Patent provides an individual or an organization exclusive rights which enable them to protect their concept or idea from being used by someone else. The patent rights are there for a particular period of time; after which any other person or organizations are free to use the concept or idea.

If during these specified period if someone else tries to use the technique for their own benefit then it is illegal and the patentee can take legal action against the offender. However, if anyone tries to use the patentee's concept, product or technique to make profits then this is termed a patent infringement.

This is why it is always advised that those who are applying for the patent should go for patent search. Patent search helps to provide and individual with an idea that whether the product for which he is seeking patent is already patented or not. Patent search can be done in different ways. There are today online sites where the patent search can be done; these online sites will provide the lists of the entire patent from all over the world.

The respective patent office in each country has also information regarding the patents in that particular country and also about the products or concepts which have been patented all over the world. This also helps a lot in patent search.

Patent infringement means others trying to use a patentee's technique for making profit or for his personal motive without taking the consent of the patentee. It is illegal and the patentee has all the rights to take legal action against those persons or organization.

So, if a proper patent search has been done then the chances of patent infringement is minimized.

Different countries have different laws to deal with the infringement but every country tries to protect the right of the patentee. The patentee may too provide various excuses as to why he did resort to such an illegal procedure. They may try to prove that the patentee has adopted illegal means to obtain patent rights and at the time of filing the application that particular method or technique were already being used by some others.

The most important thing is that the application must be properly prepared because complete application which presents the case strongly goes a long way in ensuring that the applicant is granted the patent. So, a patentee should carefully prepare the patent application.

Before filing for patent, an applicant should do proper patent search and should confirm from all the sources that his product is unique and has not been patented. After properly verifying he should go for filing the application for patent.

This will help him or her to avoid any trouble which would have otherwise created problem.

Chapter 6: How To Get A Patent

If you think that you have invented something useful and you don't want others to steal or copy then you should file a patent application. All your hard work will be wasted if you don't get a patent. You should not publicize your invention until you get a patent.

A patent is a promise made by the government of any country to protect your invention and to provide you with some exclusive rights, such as you can make, sell or use the patented item.

It is the best way to protect your invention from unauthorized usage. You can then take legal action against the person who tries to copy your invention in any form. If you don't apply for a patent then anyone can copy your invention and easily make money out of it. If you don't have adequate information on how to get a patient then it is indeed a difficult job. To get a patent you should apply for it. Each country has its own procedure of issuing a patent.

You can also hire a lawyer who specializes in patent laws, in case you don't have the slightest idea about how to get a patent. Many inventors have successfully obtained patents without taking the help of lawyers.

To get a patent your invention must be new and useful. You should prove that your invention works. Every invention cannot be patented. You should determine whether your project is commercially viable. These are the prerequisites to acquire a patent. Your invention should qualify for a patent.

You should keep a record of your invention. Note down every step of your invention process. Describe every aspect of your invention. You should also build a prototype of your invention and test it if possible. All these efforts should be documented. Make sure that your invention meets all requirements for getting a patent.

You can either apply for a regular patent or a provisional patent. The next step is to file a patent application. You may have to spend some time and money for filling a patent. To get a patent application you have to submit patent application and pay the application fees. Unless your application is approved it is not possible to get a patent.

Research the rules and regulations pertaining to patent. Familiarity with patent laws will help you to get a patent. Unfamiliarity with these laws will take you many years to get a patent

If you are not familiar with the laws, you can always take the help of internet. If you don't have the time to complete the necessary paper work then you must consult a lawyer.

If you want an international patent then select those areas where you will have no problem in marketing your invention.

Chapter 7: Steps Of Getting A Patent

A patent can be described as an invention that is granted by a government and the creator of such patent is conferred with the sole rights in regards with the usage, making and selling of the invention. After a certain thing is invented the creator of this invention, needs to go through a procedure to get this patent on a technology or a product. There are various steps of getting a patent and numerous reasons for getting the same.

These steps of getting a patent are not easy and need to be done through a proper and procedure. This procedure involves a legal process, which is quite inevitable, and involves spending a lot of money. But for the people who cannot afford to pay these big amounts can secure their patents by themselves as well. The Federal Law has authorized the U.S Patent and Trademark Office (USPTO) to assist those people who have applied for patents without the help of their lawyers.

But for the people who can hire a patent lawyer can follow the steps of getting a patent that are prescribed by the attorney thus making you tension free as the patent will go through a legal process. The vital steps of getting a patent are that you should be sure that your invention fits the parameters for a patent and justifies all the criteria's of the invention.

The steps of getting a patent are obligatory for every inventor and the procedure may take a little long than expected. However, with these steps it will be easier to obtain long awaited results.

Following are the necessary steps of getting a patent. It is necessary for the inventor to keep a detailed proof of the invention. It is mandatory to put the date and sign each entry and keep two responsible people to sign these documents. At the same time it is also necessary to know that if your invention matches the parameters of the Patent and Trademark office's board of categories.

Steps of getting a patent include a thorough survey of the market that you wish to enter. One of the most important steps of getting a patent is that the inventor needs to prove that there was no prior effort done for such kind of invention. Last but not the least the inventor needs to make an application to the USPTO to be eligible to qualify for the legal procedure.

With all these steps of getting a patent, you can get your invention on a technology or as a product.

Chapter 8: Using An Agent When Applying For A Patent

Today we are living in a technology era where every other day a new invention or new discovery takes place. New technology, new invention and new gadgets are constantly being developed.

Patents provide exclusive rights to inventors to protect their invention from being used by others for a specific period of time. Today constant up gradation of existing technology and invention of new technology has become very common.

Earlier, in spite of hard work the discoverers had to suffer because their products or concepts were being utilized by others for making money. This disheartened them. In order to protect the interests of these individuals patents were introduced.

A patent can help individuals, companies and even countries that otherwise would have been at disadvantage. For a particular specified period the rights are completely exclusives so these inventors can use it for business purpose and can make fortunes. Patents are of different types like chemical patent, biological patent, software patent business method patent, petty patent or innovation patent, design patent and plant patent.

Today each nation has their own patent office which is responsible for granting patents to the discoverer. The inventor is provided with an application form at the patent office; in the application form he or she has to furnish all the relevant details about his invention; the purpose and the usefulness of the discovery should be outlined exhaustively; the inventor may even be required to use illustrative diagrams to put forth his point.

Anyone who wants to patent their product or technology could get in touch with a patent agent. These agents are authorized by the government and have got rights to help the applicant in patenting his or her product. Those desirous of obtaining patent are required to make their invention public. While doing so the applicant constantly takes advice of the patent agent.

These patent agents provide all kinds" legal advice and other related advice to the applicant. These agents have to first register themselves at the patent office; the procedure for registration may vary from country to country. Whenever in problem, the applicant or even those who have been awarded patent can seek the help of patent agent.

Patents have also been the cause of major disputes. If the dispute is confined to a national boundary then the respective country's patent office can intervene and take steps to protect the rights of the inventor. But when the disputer crosses the national boundaries then matter becomes too difficult to handle.

Understanding the complexities of international disputes; countries are making concerted efforts to bring all patent laws under a single jurisdiction such as bringing it under the ambit of World Trade Organization.

Paris Convention for the Protection of Industrial Property,

European Patent Convention, European Patent Organization, and Patent Cooperation are some of the other international forums which are actively trying towards resolving international disputes with regard to patents.

Patent agents are of great help and have helped many to solve complex problems related to patents. However, an individual should verify the credentials of the agents before seeking their help.

Chapter 9: Patent Laws

In absence of physical boundaries, knowledge and idea free flows, uninterrupted and unhindered, from one place to the other place. An incident in one corner of the world affects people residing in any other part of the world.

In this knowledge era people are constantly engaged in designing new masterpiece of their own. New inventions, new technology and new gadgets are regularly being introduced in the market.

However, since knowledge flows very fast there are umpteen chances of the knowledge being copied by others for some business purpose. This might be harmful for the discoverer because he had toiled hard to discover the new technology but at the end of the day he finds someone else making fortunes of his hard work.

Efforts are being made to bring all patent laws under a single jurisdiction such as bringing it under the ambit of World Trade Organization. TRIPs Agreement was a move aimed in this direction and hopefully have also achieved success.

The Constitution of the United States gives Congress the power to enact laws relating to patents, in Article I, section 8, which reads "Congress shall have power to promote the progress of science and useful arts, by securing for limited times to authors and inventors the exclusive right to their respective writings and discoveries." Under this power Congress has from time to time enacted various laws relating to patents. The first patent law was enacted in 1790. The law now in effect is a general revision which was enacted July 19, 1952, and which came into effect January 1, 1953. It is codified in Title 35, United States Code.

The patent law specifies the subject matter for which a patent may be obtained and the conditions for patentability. The law establishes the Patent and Trademark Office for administering the law relating to the granting of patents, and contains various other provisions relating to patents.

What Can Be Patented?

The patent law specifies the general field of subject matter that can be patented and the conditions under which a patent may be obtained.

In the language of the statute, any person who "invents or discovers any new and useful process, machine, manufacture, or composition of matter, or any new and useful improvements thereof, may obtain a patent" subject to the conditions and requirements of the law. The word "process" is defined as process or method, and new processes, primarily industrial or technical processes that may be patented. The term "machine" used in the statute needs no explanation. The term "manufacture" refers to articles which are made, and includes all manufactured articles. The term "composition of matter" relates to chemical compositions and may include mixtures of ingredients as well as new chemical compounds. These classes of subject matter taken together include practically everything which is made by man and the process for making them.

The Atomic Energy Act of 1954 excludes the patenting of inventions useful solely in the utilization of special nuclear material or atomic energy for atomic weapons.

The patent law specifies that the subject matter must be "useful." The term "useful" in this connection refers to the condition that the subject matter has a useful purpose and also may be operative, that is, a machine which will not operate to perform the intended purpose would not be called useful, and therefore would not be granted a patent.

Interpretations of the statute by the courts have defined the limits of the field of subject matter which can be patented, thus it has been held that methods of doing business and printed matter cannot be patented.

In the case of mixtures of ingredients, such as medicines, a patent cannot be granted unless there is more to the mixture than the effect of its components. (So called patent medicines are ordinarily not patented, the phrase "patent medicine" in this connection does not have the meaning that the medicine is patented) A patent cannot be obtained upon a mere idea or suggestion. The patent is granted upon the new medicine, manufacture, and not upon the idea or suggestion of the new medicine. A complete description of the actual medicine or other subject matter sought to be patented is required.

Chapter 10: Novelty And Other Conditions For Obtaining A Patent.

In order for an invention to be patentable it must be new as defined in the patent law, which provides that an invention cannot be patented if-

(a) The invention was known or used by others in United State, or patented or described in a printed publication in United State or a foreign country, before the invention thereof by the applicant for patent, or

(b) The invention was patented or described in a printed publication in the US or a foreign country or in public use or on sale in Unites State more than one year prior to the application for patent in the United States...."

If the invention has been described in a printed publication anywhere in the world, or if it has been in public use or on sale in United State before the date that the applicant made his invention, a patent cannot be obtained. If the invention has been described in a printed publication anywhere, or has been in public use or on sale in United State more than one year before the date on which an application for patent is filed, a valid patent cannot be obtained.

In this connection it is immaterial when the invention was made, or whether the printed publication or public use was by the inventor himself or by someone else. If the inventor describes the invention in a printed publication or uses the invention publicly, or places it on sale, he must apply for a patent before one year has gone by, otherwise any right to a patent will be lost.

Even if the subject matter sought to be patented is not exactly shown by the prior art, and involves one or more differences over the most nearly similar thing already known, a patent may still be refused if the differences would be obvious. The subject matter sought to be patented must be sufficiently different from what has been used or described before so that it may be said to be indistinct to a person having ordinary skill in the area of technology related to the invention. For example, the substitutions of one material for another, or changes in size, are ordinarily not allowed a patent.

Chapter 11: The United States Patent And Trademark Office

Congress established the United States Patent and Trademark Office to issue patents on behalf of the Government. The Patent and Trademark Office as a distinct bureau may be said to date from the year 1802 when a separate official in the Department of State who became known as "Superintendent of Patents" was placed in charge of patents. The revision of the patent laws enacted in 1836 reorganized the Patent and Trademark Office and designated the official in charge as Commissioner of Patents and Trademarks. The Patent and Trademark Office remained in the Department of State until 1849 when it was transferred to the Department of Interior. In 1925 it was transferred to the Department of Commerce where it is today.

The Patent and Trademark Office administers the patent laws as they relate to the granting of patents for inventions, and performs other duties relating to patents. It examines applications for patents to determine if the applicants are entitled to patents under the law and grants the patents when they are so entitled; it publishes issued patents and various publications concerning patents, records assignments of patents, maintains a search room for the use of the public to examine issued patents and records, supplies copies of records and other papers, and the like. Similar functions are performed with respect to the registration of trademarks. The Patent and Trademark Office has no jurisdiction over questions of infringement and the enforcement of patents, nor over matters relating to the promotion or utilization of patents or inventions.

The head of the Office is the Assistant Secretary and Commissioner of Patents and Trademarks and his staff includes the Deputy Assistant Secretary and Deputy Commissioner, several assistant commissioners, and other officials. As head of the Office, the Commissioner superintends or performs all duties with respect to the granting and issuing of patents and the registration of trademarks; exercises general supervision over the entire work of the Patent and Trademark Office; prescribes the rules, subject to the approval of the Secretary of Commerce, for the conduct of proceedings in the Patent and Trademark Office and for recognition of attorneys and agents; administers judgment of various questions (brought before him by petition as prescribed by the rules, and performs other duties (necessary and required) for the administration of the Patent and Trademark Office.

The work of examining applications for patents is divided among a number of examining groups, each group having jurisdiction over certain assigned fields of technology. Each group is headed by a group director and staffed by a number of examiners. The examiners review applications for patents and determine whether patents can be granted.

An appeal can be taken to the Board of Patent Appeals and Interference from their decisions refusing to grant a patent and a review by the Commissioner of Patents and Trademarks may be had on other matters by petition. The examiners also identify applications that claim the same invention and initiate proceedings, known as interference, to determine who was the first inventor.

In addition to the examining groups, other offices perform various services, such as receiving and distributing mail, receiving new applications, handling sales of printed copies of patents, making copies of records, inspecting drawings, and recording assignments.

At present, the Patent and Trademark Office has about 4,400 employees, of whom about half are examiners and others with technical and legal training. Patent applications are received at the rate of over 170,000 per year. The Patent and Trademark Office receives over five million pieces of mail each year.

Chapter 12: Publications Of The Patent And Trademark Office

The specification and accompanying drawings of all patents are published on the same day they are granted and printed copies are sold to the public by the Patent and Trademark Office. Over 8 million patents issued by the U.S. Patent Office. "Patent No. 7 million was issued on Valentine's Day 2006 to John P. O'Brien at the DuPont Co. for cotton-like, biodegradable "polysaccharide fibers polysaccharide fibers" used in textile applications.

Printed copies of any patent, identified by its patent number, may be purchased from the Patent and Trademark Office. Future patents classified in subclasses containing subject matter of interest may be obtained, as they issue, by prepayment of a deposit and a service charge. For the cost of such subscription service, a separate inquiry should be sent to the Patent and Trademark Office.

The Official Gazette of the United States Patent and Trademark Office is the official journal relating to patents and trademarks. It has been published weekly since January 1872 (replacing the old "Patent Office Reports"), and is now issued each Tuesday in two parts, one describing patents and the other trademarks. It contains a claim and a selected figure of the drawings of each patent granted on that day; notices of patent and trademark suits; indexes of patents and patentees, list of patents available for license or sale; and much general information such as orders, notices, changes in rules, changes in classification, etc. The Official Gazette is sold on subscription and by single copies by the Superintendent of Documents, U.S. Government Printing Office, Washington, D. C. 20402.

The illustrations and claims of the patents are arranged in the Official Gazette according to the Patent and Trademark Office classification of subject matter, permitting ready reference to patents in any particular field. Street addresses of patentees and a geographical index of residents of inventors are included. Copies of the Official Gazette may be found in public libraries of larger cities.

Index of Patents: This annual index to the Official Gazette is currently in two volumes, one an index of patentees and the other an index by subject matter of the patents. Sold by Superintendent of Documents.

Index of Trademarks: An annual index of registrants of trademarks. Sold by Superintendent of Documents.

Manual of Classification: A loose-leaf book containing a list of all the classes and subclasses of inventions in the Patent and Trademark Office classification systems, a subject matter index, and other information relating to classification. Substitute pages are issued from time to time. Annual subscription includes the basic manual and substitute pages. Sold by Superintendent of Documents.

Classification Definitions: Contains the changes in classification of patents as well as definitions of new and revised classes and subclasses. Sold by Patent and Trademark Office.

Title 37 Code of Federal Regulations: Includes rules of practice for Patents, Trademarks and Copyrights. Available from the Superintendent of Documents.

Basic Facts about Trademarks: Contains general information for the layman about applications for, and registration of, trademarks and service marks. Copies may be purchased from Superintendent of Documents.

Directory of Registered Patent Attorneys and Agents Arranged by States and Countries: An alphabetical and geographical listing of patent attorneys and agents registered to practice before the U.S. Patent and Trademark Office. Sold by Superintendent of Documents.

Manual of Patent Examining Procedure: A loose-leaf manual which serves primarily as a detailed reference work on patent examining practice and procedure for the Patent and Trademark Office's Examining Corps. Subscriptions service includes basic manual, quarterly revisions, and change notices. Sold by Superintendent of Documents.

The Story of the United States Patent Office: A chronological account of the development of the U.S. Patent and Trademark Office and patent system and of inventions which had unusual impact on the American economy and society. Sold by Superintendent of Documents.

Chapter 13: General Information And Correspondence

All business with the Patent and Trademark Office should be transacted by writing to "COMMISSIONER OF PATENTS AND TRADEMARKS, WASHINGTON, D. C. 20231." Correspondents should be sure to include their full return addresses, including Zip Codes.

Applicants and attorneys are required to conduct their business with decorum and courtesy. Papers presented in violation of this requirement will be returned.

Separate letters (but not necessarily in separate envelopes) should be written in relation to each distinct subject of inquiry, such as assignments, payments, orders for printed copies of patents, orders for copies of records, requests for other services, etc. None of these should be included with letters responding to Office actions in applications.

When a letter concerns a patent application, the correspondent must include the serial number, filing date and Group Art Unit number. When a letter concerns a patent, it must include the name of the patentee, the title of the invention, the patent number and the date of issue.

An order for a copy of an assignment must give the book and page or reel and frame of the record, as well as the name of the inventor; otherwise, an additional charge is made for the time consumed in making the search for the assignment.
Applications for patents are not open to the public, and no information concerning them is released except on written

authority of the applicant, his assignee, or his attorney, or when necessary to the conduct of the business of the Office. Patents and related records, including records of any decisions, the records of assignments other than those relating to assignments of patent applications, books, and other records and papers in the Office are open to the public. They may be inspected in the Patent and Trademark Office Search Room or copies may be ordered.

The Office cannot respond to inquiries concerning the novelty and patentability of an invention in advance of the filing of an application; give advice as to possible infringement of a patent; advise of the propriety of filing an application; respond to inquiries as to whether or to whom any alleged invention has been patented; act as an expounder of the patent law or as counselor for individuals, except in deciding questions arising before it in regularly filed cases. Information of a general nature may be furnished either directly or by supplying or calling attention to an appropriate publication.

Library, Search Room Searches And Patent And Trademark Depositor Libraries

The Scientific and Technical Information Center of the Patent and Trademark Office at Crystal Plaza 3, 2021 Jefferson Davis Highway, Arlington, Va., has available for public use over 120,000 volumes of scientific and technical books in various languages, about 90,000 bound volumes of periodicals devoted to science and technology, the official journals of 77 foreign patent organizations, and over 12 million foreign patents.

A Search Room is provided where the public may search and examine United States patents granted since 1836. Patents are arranged according to the Patent and Trademark Office classification system of over 400 classes and over 120,000 subclasses. By searching in these classified patents, it is possible to determine, before actually filing an application, whether an invention has been anticipated by a United States patent, and it is also possible to obtain the information contained in patents relating to any field of endeavour. The Search Room contains a set of United States patents arranged in numerical order and a complete set of the Official Gazette.

A Files Information Room also is maintained where the public may inspect the records and files of issued patents and other open records. Applicants, their attorneys or agents, and the general public are not entitled to use the records and files in the examiners' rooms.

The Search Room is open from 8 a.m. to 8 p.m. Monday through Friday except on Federal holidays. Since a patent is not always granted when an application is filed, many inventors attempt to make their own investigation before applying for a patent. This may be done in the Search Room of the Patent and Trademark Office, and libraries, located throughout the U.S., which have been designated as Patent and Trademark Depository Libraries (PTDL). Patent attorneys or agents may be employed to make a so-called preliminary search through the prior United States patents to discover if the particular device or one similar to it has been shown in some prior patent. This search is not always as complete as that made by the Patent and Trademark

Office during the examination of an application, but only serves, as its name indicates a preliminary purpose. For this reason, the Patent and Trademark Office examiner may, and often does, reject claims in an application on the basis of prior patents or publications not found in the preliminary search.

Those who cannot come to the Search Room may order from the Patent and Trademark Office copies of lists of original patents or of cross-referenced patents contained in the subclasses comprising the field of search, or may inspect and obtain copies of the patents at a Patent and Trademark Depository Library. The Patent and Trademark Depository Libraries (PTDLs) receive current issues of U. S. Patents and maintain collections of earlier issued patents and trademark information. The scope of these collections varies from library to library, ranging from patents of only recent years to all or most of the patents issued since 1790.

These patent collections are open to public use. Each of the Patent and Trademark Depository Libraries, in addition, offers the publications of the U.S. Patent Classification System (e. g. The Manual of Classification, Index to the U.S. Patent Classification, Classification Definitions, etc.) and other patent documents and forms, and provides technical staff assistance in their use to aid the public in gaining effective access to information contained in patents. The collections are organized in patent number sequence.

Available in all PTDLs is the Classification and Search Support Information System (CASSIS), computer data base. With various modes, it permits the effective identification of appropriate classifications to search, provides numbers of patents assigned to a classification to permit finding the patents in a numerical file of patents, provides the current classification(s) of all patents, permits word searching on classification titles, abstracts, the Index provides certain bibliographic information on more recently issued patents.

Facilities for making paper copies from either microfilm in reader printers or from the bound volumes in paper-to-paper copies are generally provided for a fee.

Due to variations in the scope of patent collections among the Patent and Trademark Depository Libraries and in their hours of service to the public, anyone contemplating the use of the patents at a particular library is advised to contact that library, in advance, about its collection and hours, so as to avert possible inconvenience.

State Name of Library
- Alabama Auburn University Libraries
- Birmingham Public Library
- Alaska Anchorage: Z. J. Loussac Public Library
- Arizona Tempe:Noble Library, Arizona State University
- Arkansas Little Rock: Arkansas State University
- California Los Angeles City Library
- Sacramento: California State Library
- San Diego Public Library
- Sunnyvale Patent Clearinghouse
- Colorado Denver Public Library
- Connecticut New Haven: Science Park Library

- Delaware Newark: University of Delaware Library
- District of Columbia Washington: Howard University
- Florida Fort Lauderdale: Broward County Main Library
- Miami- Dade Public Library
- Orlando: University of Central Florida Libraries
- Tampa: Tampa Campus Library University of South Florida
- Georgia Atlanta: Price Gilbert Memorial Library, Georgia Institute of Technology
- Hawaii Honolulu: Hawaii State Public Library System
- Idaho Moscow: Library University of Idaho
- Illinois Chicago Public Library
- Springfield: Illinois State Library
- Indiana Indianapolis-Marion County Public Library
- West Lafayette: Siegesmund Engineering Laboratory, Purdue University
- Iowa Des Moines: State Library of Iowa
- Kansas Wichita: Ablah Library, Wichita State University
- Kentucky Louisville Free Public Library
- Louisiana Baton Rouge: Troy H. Middleton Library, Louisiana State
- Maryland College Park: Engineering and Physical Sciences Library University of Maryland
- Massachusetts Amherst: Physical Sciences Library, University of Massachusetts
- Boston Public Library
- Michigan Am Arbor: Engineering Library,

- University of Michigan Big Rapids: Abigail S. Timme Library
- Ferris State University
- Detroit Public Library,
- Minnesota Minneapolis Public Library and Information Center
- Mississippi Jackson: Mississippi Library Commission
- Missouri Kansas City: Linda Hall Library
- St. Louis Public Library
- Montana Butte: Montana College of Mineral Science and Technology Library
- Nebraska Lincoln: Engineering Library, University of Nebraska- Lincoln
- Nevada Reno: University of Nevada-Reno Library
- New Hampshire Durham: University of New Hampshire Library
- New Jersey Newark Public Library
- Piscataway: Library of Science and Medicine, Rutgers University
- New Mexico Albuquerque: University of New Mexico
- General Library New York Albany: New York State Library
- Buffalo and Erie County Public Library
- New York Public Library (The Research Libraries)
- North Carolina Raleigh: D. H. Hill Library, North Carolina
- State University North Dakota Grand Forks: Chester Fritz Library,

- University of North Dakota Ohio Cincinnati and Hamilton County, Public Library of Cleveland
- Public Library Columbus: Ohio State
- University Toledo/Lucas County Public Library
- Oklahoma Stillwater Oklahoma State University Center for International Trade Development
- Oregon Salem: Oregon State Library
- Pennsylvania Philadelphia: The Free Library of Pittsburgh Carnegie Library of University Park
- Pattee Library, Pennsylvania State University
- Rhode Island Providence Public Library
- South Carolina Charleston: Medical University of South Carolina
- Clemson University Libraries
- Tennessee Memphis and Shelby County Public Library and Information Center
- Nashville: Stevenson Science Library, Vanderbilt
- Texas Austin: McKinney Engineering Library, University of Texas at Austin
- College Station: Sterling C. Evans Library, Texas A & M University
- Dallas Public Library Houston: The Fondren Library, Rice University
- Utah Salt Lake City: Marriott Library, University
- of Utah
- Virginia Richmond: James Branch Cabell Library, Virginia Commonwealth University
- Washington Seattle: Engineering Library, University of Washington
- West Virginia Morgantown: Evansdale Library, West Virginia University

- Wisconsin Madison: Kurt F. Wendt Library, University of Wisconsin Madison Milwaukee Public Library

Chapter 14: Be Legally Protected

An inventor needs a patent, just like a composer and a writer needs a copyright, and a company needs a trademark.

Patent lawyers are licentiate to assist as inventor's representation during the prosecution proceedings of the patent. Patent attorneys create patent applications and help the inventor while on the process of patent prosecution.

These attorneys are adequately trained in the technological area, often either engineering or science and passed an examination supervised by the PTO which rates an attorney's knowledge of patent law. Yet, patent attorneys should also have a law degree and are able to help the patent holder in legal and official proceedings such as infringements to help advocate their rights.

Patent attorneys are adept in preparing and pursuing a patent application via the USPTO or the U.S. Patent and Trademark Office. This sector normally considers patent agents as good as patent lawyers, in the condition that they are officially registered.

Since the United States Court of Appeals for the Federal Circuit is an ordinary legitimate forum used to report patent infringement, patent attorneys may also select to impose copyright, trademark, or patent laws in a federal court or state. A plaintiff may accept restrictive relief or financial damages from an individual who made use of a copyright, trademark, or patent in an illegal fashion, by going to any court aside from the Court of Appeals.

There are several resources existing to help you search for a right patent agent or attorney, such as trade associations, the Internet, as well as district legal organizations. However, a great initial patent source stop is the USPTO's site. The web site presents a master list of attorneys and agents licensed to carry out their practices before the office.

More so, a patent attorney should of course have a law background and shall be acknowledged to the bar in single or more legal authorities. Currently, the U.S. has a duel system for patent attorneys and agents. There are roughly 22600 active patent lawyers and 7200 active agents registered to exercise legal professions before the USPTO office, thus the inventor has an important quantity of both kinds of patent practitioners to be evaluated.

A major thing that an inventor should remember when choosing either a patent attorney or patent agent is to pick one entailing enough experience in the invention field. As a universal rule, the patent attorney normally has greater fees than the patent agent due to the attorney's extra educational background.

One who has an experience in the field of invention can be much more competent and is able to create an effective patent application. There are various ways to select a patent attorney. One technique is the usage of referrals by dealing with individuals and other inventors who practice in the invention field. Another method helpful in searching a patent attorney is to browse on the database of registered practitioners created by USPTO. An ideal search sort is to begin with your local area given that it is most of the time easier to assess probable patent attorneys through telephone calls preceded by a personal meeting that is definitely much price effective on a local source.

Patent attorneys may conduct patent related court litigations or exercise certain services that are permitted by the local authority as practicing or performing law. For instance, a patent lawyer can make a contract recounting a patent, for example a license or an assignment, only if he resides in a state that deems contract drafting as practicing law.

As a rundown, patent attorneys have proficiency in helping inventors acquire an IP or intellectual property protection of their inventions and their own ideas. People claiming of being patent attorneys should have passed the so-called Patent Bar Examination. For them to qualify for the Bar, patent attorneys should have a college degree in a certified technical course like engineering, or in the field of science like chemistry or biology. Patent attorneys shall incessantly update their learning of IP concerns. Few websites provide specifics on the Patent Bar Examination.

May it be a copyright, patent, or trademark, a patent attorney can do it all. Name it and you will surely have it. But still, remember to pick the right one.

Chapter 15: Attorneys And Agents

The preparation of an application for patent and the conducting of the proceedings in the Patent and Trademark Office to obtain the patent is an undertaking requiring the knowledge of patent law and Patent and Trademark Office practice as well as knowledge of the scientific or technical matters involved in the particular invention. Inventors may prepare their own applications and file them in the Patent and Trademark Office and conduct the proceedings themselves, but unless they are familiar with these matters or study them in detail, they may get into considerable difficulty. While a patent may be obtained in many cases by persons not skilled in this work, there would be no assurance that the patent obtained would adequately protect the particular invention.

Most inventors employ the services of registered patent attorneys or patent agents. The law gives the Patent and Trademark Office the power to make rules and regulations governing conduct and the recognition of patent attorneys and agents to practice before the Patent and Trademark Office. Persons who are not recognized by the Patent and Trademark Office for this practice are not permitted by law to represent inventors before the Patent and Trademark Office. The Patent and Trademark Office maintains a register of attorneys and agents. To be admitted to this register, a person must comply with the regulations prescribed by the Office, which require a showing that the person is of good moral character and of good repute and that he/she has the legal and scientific and technical qualifications necessary to render applicants for patents a valuable service. Certain of these qualifications must be demonstrated by the passing of an examination. Those admitted to the examination must have a college degree in engineering or physical science or the equivalent of such a degree. The Patent and Trademark Office registers both attorneys at law and persons who are not attorneys at law. The former persons are now referred to as "patent attorneys" and the latter persons are referred to as "patent agents." Insofar as the work of preparing an application for patent and conducting the prosecution in the Patent and Trademark Office is concerned, patent agents are usually just as well qualified as patent attorneys, although patent agents cannot conduct patent litigation in the courts or perform various services which the local jurisdiction considers as practicing law. For example, a patent agent could not draw up a contract relating to a patent, such as an assignment or a license, if the State in which he resides considers drawing contracts as practicing law.

Some individuals and organizations that are not registered advertise their services in the fields of patent searching and invention marketing and development. Such individuals and organizations cannot represent inventors before the Patent and Trademark Office. They are not subject to Patent and Trademark Office discipline, and the Office cannot assist inventors in dealing with them.

The Patent and Trademark Office cannot recommend any particular attorney or agent, or aid in the selection of an attorney or agent, as by stating, in response to inquiry that a named patent attorney, agent, or firm, is "reliable" or capable." The Patent and Trademark Office publishes a directory of all registered patent attorneys and agents who have indicated their availability to accept new clients, arranged by states, cities, and foreign countries. The Directory must be purchased from the Government Printing Office.

The telephone directories of most large cities have, in the classified section, a heading for patent attorney's under which those in that area are listed. Many large cities have associations of patent attorneys.

In employing a patent attorney or agent, the inventor executes a power of attorney or authorization of agent which must be filed in the Patent and Trademark Office and is usually a part of the application papers. When an attorney has been appointed, the Office does not communicate with the inventor directly but conducts the correspondence with the attorney since he/she is acting for the inventor thereafter, although the inventor is free to contact the Patent and Trademark Office concerning the status of his/her application. The inventor may remove the attorney or agent by revoking the power of authorization.

The Patent and Trademark Office has the power to disbar, or suspend from practicing before it, persons guilty of gross misconduct, etc., but this can only be done after a full hearing with the presentation of clear and convincing evidence concerning the misconduct. The Patent and Trademark Office will receive and, in appropriate cases, act upon complaints against attorneys and agents. The fees charged by patent attorneys and agents for their professional services are not subject to regulation by the

Patent and Trademark Office. Definite evidence of overcharging may afford basis for Patent and Trademark Office action, but the Office rarely intervenes in disputes concerning fees.

Disclosure Document:

One of the services provided for inventors is the acceptance and preservation for a two year period of papers disclosing an invention. This disclosure is accepted as evidence of the dates of conception of the invention. It will be retained for two years at which time it will be destroyed unless it is referred to in a separate letter in a related patent application.

A fee must accompany the disclosure. See current fee schedule. The disclosure is limited to written matter or drawings on paper or other thin, flexible material, such as linen or plastic drafting material, having dimensions or being folded to dimensions not to exceed 8-1/2 x 13 inches (21.6 by 33.0 cm). Photographs are acceptable. Each page should be numbered. Text and drawings should be of such quality as to permit reproduction.

The disclosure must be accompanied by a stamped, self-addressed envelope and a duplicate copy also signed by the inventor. The papers will be stamped with an identifying number and returned with the reminder that the Disclosure Document may be relied upon only as evidence of the date of conception and that an application must be filed in order to provide patent protection.

Chapter 16: Who May Apply For A Patent

According to the law, only the inventor may apply for a patent, with certain exceptions. If a person who is not the inventor should apply for a patent, the patent, if it were obtained, would be invalid. The person applying in such a case who falsely states that he/she is the inventor would also be subject to criminal penalties. If the inventor is dead, the application may be made by legal representatives, that is, the administrator or executor of the estate. If the inventor is insane, the application for patent may be made by a guardian. If an inventor refuses to apply for a patent or cannot be found, a joint inventor or a person having a proprietary interest in the invention may apply on behalf of the missing inventor.

If two or more persons make an invention jointly, they apply for a patent as joint inventors. A person who makes a financial contribution is not a joint inventor and cannot be joined in the application as an inventor. It is possible to correct an innocent mistake in erroneously omitting an inventor or erroneously naming a person as an inventor.

Officers and employees of the Patent and Trademark Office are prohibited by law from applying for a patent or acquiring, directly or indirectly, except by inheritance or bequest, any patent or any right or interest in any patent.

Chapter 17: Application For Patent

To patent a product, one has to submit an application in the patent office; upon verification the application is either accepted or rejected. In the application the applicant provides detail about his invention and makes claim that he should be given patent of the product or concept which he has invented.

Generally the application is filed in the patent office which falls under the jurisdiction of the applicant which in majority of the cases is the country in which the applicant is residing. However there are regional forums also like European Patent Office where also the application can be filed.

The applicant has to go through the process of patent prosecution wherein he has to interact with the patent office as why he should be granted patent of the respective product. The applicant has to put forth strong argument he or she should prove that the invention which he is claiming to be his own is beneficial to the society and if patent is granted to him then this won't become a stumbling block in the invention of the new product. There is also patent litigation which deals with the legal aspects of the patent.

There are different types of patents such as plant patents, software patents, design patents and utility patents. Patent office also contains different types of application which can be used for different purposes.

Standard application format is available in the patent office wherein the applicant provides all the details about his invention and strongly argues for the patent. After proper verification he may or may not be granted the patent of the product. The provisional patent application is also one of the ways by which one can apply for the patent. The concept was introduced in the United States of America on June 8, 1995. This is in fact first filing for the patent; it is also cheap.

If someone is interested in continuing with the patent then they could go for filing a standard patent application. Some patent offices allows for continuation of the previous patent application. The continuous application process can be either in parts or in full depending on the applicant's desire.

In the case of the divisional application the existing application is divided into various parts but while doing do the original date of the filing of the application remains intact.

The most important thing is that the application must be properly prepared because complete application which presents the case strongly goes a long way in ensuring that the applicant is granted the patent.

So, a patentee should carefully prepare the patent application.

In the Unites State of America, an application for a patent is made to the Commissioner of Patents and Trademarks and includes:
(1) A written document which comprises a specification (description and claims), and an oath or declaration;

(2) A drawing in those cases in which a drawing is necessary;

(3) The filing fee. The specification and oath or declaration must be legibly written or printed in permanent ink on one side of the paper. The Office prefers typewriting on letter or legal size 8 to 8 1/2 by 10 1/2 to 13 inches, (20.3 to 21.6 by 26.7 to 33.0 cm) 1 1/2 or double spaced with margins of 1 inch (2.54 cm) on the left-hand side and at the top, if the papers filed are not correctly, legibly, and clearly written, the Patent and Trademark Office may require typewritten or printed papers.

The application for patent is not forwarded for examination until all its required parts, complying with the rules relating thereto, are received. If the papers and parts are incomplete, or so defective that they cannot be accepted as a complete application for examination, the applicant will be notified about the deficiencies and be given a time period in which to remedy them.

A surcharge may be required. If the applicant does not respond within the prescribed time period. The application will be returned or otherwise disposed of. The filing fee may be refunded when an application is refused acceptance as incomplete; however, a handling fee will be charged.
It is desirable that all parts of the complete application be deposited in the Office together; otherwise each part must be signed and a letter must accompany each part, accurately and clearly connecting it with the other parts of the application.

All applications are numbered in serial order, and the applicant is informed of the serial number and filing date of the application by a filing receipt. The filing date of the application is the date on which the names of the inventors, a specification (including claims) and any required drawings are received in the Patent and Trademark Office; or the date on which the last part completing the application are received in the case of a previously incomplete or defective application.

Oath Or Declaration, Signature:

The oath or declaration of the applicant is required by law. The inventor must make an oath or declaration that he/she believes himself/herself to be the original and first inventor of the subject matter of the application, and he/she must make various other allegations required by law and various allegations required by the Patent and Trademark Office rules. The oath must be sworn to by the inventor before a notary public or other officer authorized to administer oaths.

A declaration may be used in lieu of an oath as part of the original application for patent involving designs, plants, and other patentable inventions; for reissue patents; when claiming matter originally shown or described but not originally claimed; or when filing a divisional or continuing application. A declaration does not need to be notarized. The application, oath or declaration must be signed by the inventor in person, or by the person entitled by law to make application on the inventor's behalf. A full first or middle name of each inventor without abbreviation and a middle or first initial, if any, is required. The post office address of the inventor is also required.

Blank forms for applications or certain other papers are not supplied by the Patent and Trademark Office. The papers in a complete application will not be returned for any purpose whatever, nor will the filing fee be returned. If applicants have not preserved copies of the papers, the Office will furnish copies for a fee.

Filing Fees:

The filing fee of an application, except in design and plant cases, consists of a basic fee and additional fees. The basic fee entitles applicant to present twenty (20) claims, including not more than three (3) in independent forms. An additional fee is required for each claim in independent form which is in excess of three (3) and an additional fee is required for each claim (whether independent or dependent) which is in excess of a total of twenty (20) claims. If the application contains multiple dependent claims, additional fees are required.

If the owner of the invention is a small entity, (an independent inventor, a small business concern or a non-profit organization), the filing fees are reduced by half if the small entity files a verified statement. Copies of sample verification statements are enclosed.

To avoid errors in the payment of fees it is suggested that the table in the enclosed patent application transmittal letter be utilized to calculate the fee payment.

In calculating fees, a claim is in singularly dependent form if it incorporates by reference a single preceding claim which may be an independent or a dependent claim. A multiple dependent claim or any claim depending there from shall be considered as separate dependent claims in accordance with the number of claims to which reference is made.

The law also provides for the payment of additional fees on presentation of additional claims after the application is filed. When an amendment is filed which presents additional claims over the total number already paid for, or additional independent claims over the number of independent claims already accounted for, it must be accompanied by any additional fees due.

Please Note: The fees are current as of the revision date. Fees are subject to change in October each year therefore they should be verified before submission to the PTO. A fee schedule may be obtained by writing to Commissioner of Patents, Washington, D. C. 20231 -- Attention Public Service Branch.

Chapter 18: Specification (Description And Claims)

The specification must include a written description of the invention and of the manner and process of making and using it, and is required to be in such full, clear, concise, and exact terms as to enable any person skilled in the technological area to which the invention pertains, or with which it is most nearly connected, to make and use the same.

The specification must set forth the precise invention for which a patent is solicited, in such manner as to distinguish it from other inventions and from what is old. It must describe completely a specific embodiment of the process; machine, manufacture, composition of matter or improvement invented, and must explain the mode of operation or principle whenever applicable. The best mode contemplated by the inventor of carrying out his invention must be set forth.

In the case of an improvement, the specification must particularly point out the part or parts of the process, machine, manufacture, or composition of matter to which the improvement relates, and the description should be confined to the specific improvement and to such parts as necessarily cooperate with it or as may be necessary to a complete understanding or description of it.

The title of the invention, which should be as short and specific as possible, should appear as a heading on the first page of the specification, if it does not otherwise appear at the beginning of the application.

A brief abstract of the technical disclosure in the specification must be set forth in a separate page immediately following the claims in a separate paragraph under the heading "Abstract of the Disclosure." A brief summary of the invention indicating its nature and substance, which may include a statement of the object of the invention, commensurate with the invention as claimed and any object recited should precede the detailed description. Such summary should be that of the invention as claimed.

When there are drawings, there shall be a brief description of the several views of the drawings, and the detailed description of the invention shall refer to the different views by specifying the numbers of the figures, and to the different parts by use of reference numerals.

The specification must conclude with one or more claims particularly pointing out and distinctly claiming the subject matter which the applicant regards as the invention.

The claims are brief descriptions of the subject matter of the invention, eliminating unnecessary details and reciting all essential features necessary to distinguish the invention from what is old. The claims are the operative part of the patent. Novelty and patentability are judged by the claims, and, when a patent is granted, questions of infringement are judged by the courts on the basis of the claims.
When more than one claim is presented, they may be placed in dependent form in which a claim may refer back to and further restrict one or more preceding claims.

A claim in multiple dependent forms shall contain a reference, in the alternative only, to more than one claim previously set forth and then specify a further limitation of the subject matter claimed. A multiple dependent claim shall not serve as a basis for any other multiple dependent claims.

A multiple dependent claim shall be construed to incorporate by reference all the limitations of the particular claim in relation to which it is being considered.

The claim or claims must conform to the invention as set forth in the remainder of the specification and the terms and phrases used in the claims must find clear support or antecedent basis in the description so that the meaning of the terms in the claims may be ascertainable by reference to the description.

The following order of arrangement should be observed in framing the specification:
(a) Title of the invention.
(b) Cross-references to related applications, if any.
(c) Brief summary of the invention.
(d) Brief description of the several views of the drawing, if there are drawings.
(e) Detailed Description.
(f) Claim or claims.
(g) Abstract of the disclosure.

Drawing
The applicant for a patent will be required by law to furnish a drawing of the invention whenever the nature of the case

requires a drawing to understand the invention. However, the Commissioner may require a drawing where the nature of the subject matter admits of it; this drawing must be filed with the application. This includes practically all inventions except compositions of matter or processes, but a drawing may also be useful in the case of many processes.

The drawing must show every feature of the invention specified in the claims and is required by the Office rules to be in a particular form. The Office specifies the size of the sheet on which the drawing is made, the type of paper, the margins, and other details relating to the making of the drawing. The reason for specifying the standards in detail is that the drawings are printed and published in a uniform style when the patent issues and the drawings must also be such that they can be readily understood by persons using the patent descriptions.

No names or other identification will be permitted within the "sight" of the drawing, and applicants are expected to use the space above and between the hole locations to identify each sheet of drawings. This identification may consist of the attorney's name and docket number or the inventor's name and case number and may include the sheet number and the total number of sheets filed (for example, "sheet 2 of 4"). The following rule, reproduced from title 37 of the Code of Federal Regulations, relates to the standards for drawings:

Standards for drawings
(a) Paper and ink. Drawings must be made upon paper which is flexible, strong, white, smooth, non-shiny and

durable. India ink, or its equivalent in quality, is preferred for pen drawings to secure perfectly black solid lines. The use of white pigment to cover lines is not normally acceptable.

(b) Size of sheet and margins. The size of the sheets on which drawings are made may either be exactly 81/2 by 14 inches (21.6 by 35.6 cm.) or exactly 21.0 by 29.7 cm. (DIN size A4). All drawing sheets in a particular application must be the same size. One of the shorter sides of the sheet is regarded as its top.

(1) On 81/2 by 14 inch drawing sheets, the drawings must include a top margin of2 inches (5.1 cm.) and bottom and side margins of '/4 inch (6.4 mm.) from the edges, thereby leaving a "sight" precisely 8 by 113/4 inches (20.3 by 29.8 cm.). Margin border lines are not permitted. All work must be included within the "sight". The sheets may be provided with two '/4 inch (6.4 mm.) diameter holes having their centerlines spaced 11/16 inch (17.5 mm.) below the top edge and 23/4 inches (7.0 cm.) apart, said holes being equally spaced from the respective side edges.

(2) On 21.0 by 29.7 cm. drawing sheets, the drawing must include a top margin of at least 2.5 cm., a left side margin of 2.5 cm., a right side margin of 1.5 cm., and a bottom margin of 1.0 cm. Margin border lines are not permitted. All work must be contained within a sight size not to exceed 17 by 26.2 cm.

(c) Character of lines. All drawings must be made with drafting instruments or by a process which will give them satisfactory reproduction characteristics. Every line and letter must be durable, black, sufficiently dense and dark, uniformly thick and well defined; the weight of all lines and letters must be heavy enough to permit adequate reproduction. This direction applies to all lines however fine, to shading, and to lines representing cut surfaces in sectional views. All lines must be clean, sharp, and solid. Fine or crowded lines should be avoided. Solid black should not be used for sectional or surface shading. Freehand work should be avoided wherever it is possible to do so

(d) Hatching and shading.
(1) Hatching should be made by oblique parallel lines spaced sufficiently apart to enable the lines to be distinguished without difficulty.

(2) Heavy lines on the shade side of objects should preferably be used except where they tend to thicken the work and obscure reference characters. The light should come from the upper left-hand comer at an angle of 45 degrees. Surface delineation should preferably be shown by proper shading, which should be open.

(e) Scale. The scale to which a drawing is made ought to be large enough to show the mechanism without crowding when the drawing is reduced in size to two-thirds in reproduction, and views of portions of the mechanism on a larger scale should be used when necessary to show details clearly; two or more sheets should be used if one does not give sufficient room to accomplish this end, but the number of sheets should not be more than is necessary.

(f) Reference characters. The different views should be consecutively numbered figures. Reference numerals (and letters, but numerals are preferred) must be plain, legible and carefully formed, and not be encircled. They should, if possible, measure at least one-eighth of an inch (3.2 mm.) in height so that they may bear reduction to one twenty-fourth of an inch (1.1 mm.); and they may be slightly larger when there is sufficient room.

They should not be so placed in the close and complex parts of the drawing as to interfere with a thorough comprehension of the same, and therefore should rarely cross or mingle with the lines. When necessarily grouped around a certain part, they should be placed at a little distance, at the closest point where there is available space, and connected by lines with the parts to which they refer.

They should not be placed upon hatched or shaded surfaces but when necessary, a blank space may be left in the hatching or shading where the character occurs so that it shall appear perfectly distinct and separate from the work. The same part of an invention appearing in more than one view of the drawing must always be designated by the same character, and the same character must never be used to designate different parts. Reference signs not mentioned in the description shall not appear in the drawing, and vice versa.

(g) Symbols, legends. Graphical drawing symbols and other labeled and labeled representation are used must be adequately identified in the specification. While descriptive matter on drawings is not permitted, suitable legends may be used, or may be required in proper cases, as in diagrammatic views and flow sheets or to show materials or where labeled representations are employed to illustrate conventional elements. Arrows may be required, in proper cases, to show direction of movement. The lettering should be as large as, or larger than, the reference characters.

(h) [Reserved]

(i) Views. The drawing must contain as many figures as may be necessary to show the invention; the figures should be consecutively numbered if possible in the order in which they appear. The figures may be plain, elevation, section, or perspective views, and detail views of portions of elements, on a larger scale if necessary, may also be used. Exploded views, with the separated parts of the same figure embraced by a bracket, to show the relationship or order of assembly of various parts are permissible. When necessary, a view of a large machine or device in its entirety may be broken and extended over several sheets if there is no loss in facility of understanding the view.

Where figures on two or more sheets form in effect a single complete figure, the figures on the several sheets should be so arranged that the complete figure can be understood by laying the drawing sheets adjacent to one another. The arrangement should be such that no part of any of the figures appearing on the various sheets are concealed and that the complete figure can be understood even though spaces will occur in the complete figure because of the margins on the drawing sheets. The plane upon which a sectional view is taken should be indicated on the general view by a broken line, the ends of which should be designated by numerals corresponding to the figure number of the sectional view and have arrows applied to indicate the direction in which the view is taken. A moved position may be shown by a broken line superimposed upon a suitable figure if this can be done without crowding, otherwise a separate figure must be used for this purpose. Modified forms of construction can only be shown in separate figures. Views should not be connected by projection lines nor should center lines be used.

(j) **Arrangement of views.** All views on the same sheet should stand in the same direction and, if possible, stand so that they can be read with the sheet held in an upright position. If views longer than the width of the sheet are necessary for the dearest illustration of the invention, the sheet may be turned on its side so that the top of the sheet with the appropriate top margin is on the right-hand side. One figure must not be placed upon another or within the outline of another.

(k) **Figure for Official Gazette.** The drawing should, as far as possible, be so planned that one of the views will be suitable for publication in the Official Gazette as the illustration of the invention.

(l) **Extraneous matter.** Identifying indicia (such as the attorney's docket number, inventor's name, number of sheets, etc.) not to exceed 2 3/4 inches (7.0 cm.) in width may be placed in a centered location between the side edges within three-fourths inch (l9.1 mm.) of the top edge. Authorized security markings may be placed on the drawings provided they are outside the illustrations and are removed when the material is declassified. Other extraneous matter will not be permitted upon the face of a drawing.

(m) Transmission of drawings. Drawings transmitted to the Office should be sent flat, protected by a sheet of heavy binder's board, or may be rolled for transmission in a suitable mailing tube; but must never be folded. If received creased or mutilated, new drawings will be required. (See 1.152 for design drawing, 1.165 for plant drawings, and 1.174 for reissue drawings.)

The requirements relating to drawings are strictly enforced, but a drawing not complying with all of the regulations may be accepted for purpose of examination, and correction or a new drawing will be required later.

Applicants are advised to employ competent draftsmen to make their drawings.

Model, Exhibits, Specimens

Models are not required in most patent applications since the description of the invention in the specification and the drawings must be sufficiently full and complete and capable of being understood to disclose the invention without the aid of a model. A model will not be admitted unless specifically requested by the examiner.
A working model, or other physical exhibit, may be required by the Office if deemed necessary. This is not done very often. A working model may be requested in the case of applications for patent for alleged perpetual motion devices.

When the invention relates to a composition of matter, the applicant may be required to furnish specimens of the composition, or of its ingredients or intermediates, for inspection or experiment. If the invention is a micro-biological invention, a deposit of the micro-organism involved is required.

Chapter 19: Examination Of Applications And Proceedings In The Patent And Trademark Office

Applications filed in the Patent and Trademark Office and accepted as complete applications are assigned for examination to the respective examining groups having charge of the areas of technology related to the invention. In the examining group, applications are taken up for examination by the examiner to whom they have been assigned in the order in which they have been filed or in accordance with examining procedures established by the Commissioner.

Applications will not be advanced out of turn for examination or for further action except as provided by the rules, or upon order of the Commissioner to expedite the business of the Office, or upon a verified showing which, in the opinion of the Commissioner, will justify advancing them.

The examination of the application consists of a study of the application for compliance with the legal requirements and a search through United States patents, prior foreign patent documents which are available in the Patent and Trademark Office, and available literature, to see if the claimed invention is new and unobvious. A decision is reached by the examiner in the light of the study and the result of the search.

Office Action

The applicant is notified in writing of the examiner's decision by an "action" which is normally mailed to the attorney or agent. The reasons for any adverse action or any objection or requirement are stated in the action and such information or references are given as may be useful in aiding the applicant to judge the propriety of continuing the prosecution of his application.

If the invention is not considered patentable subject matter, the claims will be rejected. If the examiner finds that the invention is not new, the claims will be rejected, but the claims may also be rejected if they differ only in an obvious manner from what is found. It is not uncommon for some or all of the claims to be rejected on the first action by the examiner; relatively few applications are allowed as filed.

Applicant's Response

The applicant must request reconsideration in writing, and must distinctly and specifically point out the supposed errors in the examiner's action. The applicant must respond to every ground of objection and rejection in the prior Office action (except that a request may be made that objections or requirements as to form not necessary to further consideration of the claims be held in abeyance until allowable subject matter is indicated), and the applicant's action must appear throughout to be a bona fide attempt to advance the case to final action. The mere allegation that the examiner has erred will not be received as a proper reason for such reconsideration.

In amending an application in response to a rejection, the applicant must clearly point out why he/she thinks the amended claims are patentable in view of the state of the art disclosed by the prior references cited or the objections made. He/she must also show how the claims as amended avoid such references or objections.

After response by applicant the application will be reconsidered, and the applicant will be notified if claims are rejected, or objections or requirements made, in the same manner as after the first examination. The second Office action usually will be made final.

Final Rejection

On the second or later consideration, the rejection or other action may be made final. The applicant's response is then limited to appeal in the case of rejection of any claim and further amendment is restricted. Petition may be taken to the Commissioner in the case of objections or requirements not involved in the rejection of any claim. Response to a final rejection or action must include cancellation of, or appeal from the rejection of, each claim so rejected and, if any claim stands allowed, compliance with any requirement or objection as to form.

In making such final rejection, the examiner repeats or states all grounds of rejection then considered applicable to the claims in the application.

Interviews with examiners may be arranged, but an interview does not remove the necessity for response to Office actions within the required time, and the action of the Office is based solely on the written record.

If two or more inventions are claimed in a single application, and are regarded by the Office to be of such a nature that a single patent should not be issued for both of them, the applicant will be required to limit the application to one of the inventions. The other invention may be made the subject of a separate application which, if filed while the first application is still pending, will be entitled to the benefit of the filing date of the first application. A requirement to restrict the application to one invention may be made before further action by the examiner.

As a result of the examination by the Office, patents are granted in the case of about two out of every three applications for patents which are filed.

Amendments To Application:

Following are some details concerning amendments to the application:
The applicant may amend before or after the first examination and action as specified in the rules, or when and as specifically required by the examiner.

After final rejection or action amendments may he made canceling claims or complying with any requirement of form which has been made but the admission of any such amendment or its refusal, and any proceedings relative thereto, shall not operate to relieve the application from its condition as subject to appeal or to save it from abandonment.

If amendments touching the merits of the application are presented after final rejection, or after appeal has been taken, or when such amendment might not otherwise be proper, they may be admitted upon a showing of good and sufficient reasons why they are necessary and were not earlier presented.

No amendment can be made as a matter of right in appealed cases. After decision on appeal, amendments can only be made as provided in the rules.

The specifications, claims, and drawing must be amended and revised when required, to correct inaccuracies of description and definition of unnecessary words, and to secure correspondence between the claims, the description, and the drawing.

All amendments of the drawings or specifications, and all additions thereto, must conform to at least one of them as it was at the time of the filing of the application. Matter not found in either, involving a departure from or an addition to the original disclosure cannot be added to the application even though supported by a supplemental oath or declaration, and can be shown or claimed only in a separate application.

The claims may be amended by canceling particular claims, by presenting new claims, or by amending the language of particular claims (such amended claims being in effect new claims). In presenting new or amended claims, the applicant must point out how they avoid any reference or ground rejection of record which may be pertinent.

Erasures, additions, insertions, or alterations of the papers and records must not be made by the applicant. Amendments are made by filing a paper, directing or requesting that specified changes or additions be made. The exact word or words to be stricken out or inserted in the application must be specified and the precise point indicated where the deletion or insertion is to be made.

Amendments are "entered" by the Office by making the proposed deletions by drawing a line in red ink through the word or words canceled and by making the proposed substitutions or insertions in red ink, small insertions being written in at the designated place and larger insertions being indicated by reference.

No change in the drawing may be made except by permission of the Office. Changes in the construction shown in any drawing may be made only by submitting new drawings. A sketch in permanent ink showing proposed changes, to become part of the record, must be filed for approval by the Office before the new drawings are filed. The paper requesting amendments to the drawing should be separate from other papers.

If the number or nature of the amendments render it difficult to consider the case, or to arrange the papers' for printing or copying, the examiner may require the entire specification or claims, or any part thereof, to be rewritten.

The original numbering of the claims must be preserved throughout the prosecution. When claims are canceled, the remaining claims must not be renumbered. When claims are added by amendment or substituted for canceled claims, they must be numbered by the applicant consecutively beginning with the number next following the highest numbered claim previously presented. When the application is ready for allowance, the examiner, if necessary, will re-number the claims consecutively in the order in which they appear or in such order as may have been requested by applicant.

Time For Response And Abandonment:

The response of an applicant to an action by the Office must be made within a prescribed time limit. The maximum period for response is set at 6 months by the statute which also provides that the Commissioner may shorten the time for reply to not less than 30 days. The usual period for response to an Office action is 3 months. A shortened time for reply may be extended up to the maximum 6 months period.

An extension of time fee is normally required to be paid if the response period is extended. The amount of the fee is dependent upon the length of the extension. If no reply is received within the time period, the application is considered as abandoned and no longer pending. However, if it can be shown that the failure to prosecute was unavoidable or unintentional, the application may be revived by the Commissioner. The revival requires a petition to the Commissioner, and a fee for the petition, which should be filed without delay. The proper response must also accompany the petition if it has not yet been filed.

Chapter 20: Appeal To The Board Of Patent Appeals And Interferences To The Courts

If the examiner persists in the rejection of any of the claims in an application, or if the rejection has been made final, the applicant may appeal to the Board of Patent Appeals and Interference in the Patent and Trademark Office. The Board of Patent Appeals and Interference consists of the Commissioner of Patents and Trademarks, the Deputy Commissioner, the Assistant Commissioners, and the examiners-in-chief, but normally each appeal is heard by only three members. An appeal fee is required and the applicant must file a brief to support his/her position. An oral hearing will be held if requested upon payment of the specified fee.

As an alternative to appeal, in situations where an applicant desires consideration of different claims or further evidence, a new continuation application is often filed. The new application requires a filing fee and should submit the claims and evidence for which consideration is desired. If it is filed before expiration of the period for appeal and specific reference is made therein to the earlier application, applicant will be entitled to the earlier filing date for subject matter common to both applications.

If the decision of the Board of Patent Appeals and Interference is still adverse to the applicant, an appeal may be taken to the Court of Appeals for the Federal Circuit or a civil action may be filed against the Commissioner in the United States District court for the District of Columbia. The Court of Appeals for the Federal Circuit will review the record made in the Office and may affirm or reverse the office's action. In a civil action, the applicant may present testimony in the court, and the court will make a decision.

Interferences:

Occasionally two or more applications are filed by different inventors claiming substantially the same patentable invention. The patent can only be granted to one of them, and a proceeding known as"interference" is instituted by the Office to determine who is the first inventor and entitled to the patent. About 1 percent of the applications filed become involved in an interference proceeding. Interference proceedings may also be instituted between an application and a patent already issued, provided the patent has not been issued for more than one year prior to the filing of the conflicting application, and provided that the conflicting application is not barred from being patentable for some other reason.

Each party to such a proceeding must submit evidence of facts proving when the invention was made. In view of the necessity of proving the various facts and circumstances concerning the making of the invention during interference, inventors must be able to produce evidence to do this. If no evidence is submitted a party is restricted to the date of filing the application as his earliest date. The priority question is determined by a board of three Examiners-in-Chief on the evidence submitted. From the decision of the Board of Patent Appeals and Interference, the losing party may appeal to the Court of Appeals for the Federal Circuit or file a civil action against the winning party in the appropriate United States district court.

The terms "conception of the invention" and "reduction to practice" are encountered in connection with priority questions. Conception of the invention refers to the completion of the devising of the means for accomplishing the result. Reduction to practice refers to the actual construction of the invention in physical form; in the case of a machine it includes the actual building of the machine, in the case of an article or composition it includes the actual making of the article or composition, in the case of a process it includes the actual carrying out of the steps of the process; and actual operation, demonstration, or testing for the intended use is also usually necessary. The filing of a regular application for patent completely disclosing the invention is treated as equivalent to reduction to practice. The inventor who proves to be the first to conceive the invention and the first to reduce it to practice will be held to be the prior inventor, but more complicated situations cannot be stated this simply.

Chapter 21: Allowance And issue Of Patent

If, on examination of the application, or at a later stage during the reconsideration of the application, the patent application is found to be allowable, a notice of allowance will be sent to the applicant, or to applicant's attorney or agent, and a fee for issuing the patent is due within three months from the date of the notice.

The issue fee is due within three months after a written notice of allowance is mailed to the applicant. If timely payment is not made the application will be regarded as abandoned.

A provision is made in the statute whereby the Commissioner may accept the fee late, on a showing of unavoidable delay. When the issue fee is paid, the patent is issued as soon as possible after the date of payment, dependent upon the volume of printing on hand. The patent grant then is delivered or mailed on the day of its grant, or as soon thereafter as possible, to the inventor's attorney or agent if there is one of record, otherwise directly to the inventor. On the date of the grant, the patent file becomes open to the public. Printed copies of the specification and drawing are available on the same date.

In case the publication of an invention by the granting of a patent would be detrimental to the national defense, the patent law gives the Commissioner the power to withhold the grant of the patent and to order the invention kept secret for such period of time as the national interest requires.

Chapter 22: Nature Of Patent And Patent Rights

The patent is issued in the name of the United States under the seal of the Patent and Trademark Office, and is either signed by the Commissioner of Patents and Trademarks or has his name written thereon and attested by an Office official. The patent contains a grant to the patentee and a printed copy of the specification and drawing is annexed to the patent and forms a part of it. The grant confers "the right to exclude others from making, using or selling the invention throughout the United States" and its territories and possessions for the term of 17 years subject to the payment of maintenance fees as provided by law.

The exact nature of the right conferred must be carefully distinguished, and the key is in the words "right to exclude" in the phrase just quoted. The patent does not grant the right to make, use, or sell the invention but only grants the exclusive nature of the right. Any person is ordinarily free to make, use, or sell anything he pleases, and a grant from the Government is not necessary.

The patent only grants the right to exclude others from making, using, or selling the invention. Since the patent does not grant the right to make, use, or sell the invention, the patentee's own right to do so is dependent upon the rights of others and whatever general laws might be applicable. A patentee, merely because he or she has received a patent for an invention, is not thereby authorized to make, use or sell the invention if doing so would violate any law.

An inventor of a new automobile who has obtained a patent thereon would not be entitled to use the patented automobile in violation of the laws of a State requiring a license, nor may a patentee sell an article the sale of which may be forbidden by a law, merely because a patent has been obtained. Neither may a patentee make, use or sell his/her own invention if doing so would infringe the prior rights of others.

A patentee may not violate the Federal anti-trust laws, such as by resale price agreements or entering into combination in restraints of trade, or the pure food and drug laws, by virtue of having a patent. Ordinarily there is nothing which prohibits a patentee from making, using, or selling his/her own invention, unless he/she thereby infringes another patent which is still in force.

Since the essence of the right granted by a patent is the right to exclude others from commercial exploitation of the invention, the patentee is the only one who may make, use, or sell the invention. Others may not do so without authorization from the patentee. The patentee may manufacture and sell the invention or may license, that is, give authorization to others to do so.

The term of a patent is 17 years. A maintenance fee is due 3 1/2, 7 1/2 and 11 1/2 years after the original grant for all patents issuing from the applications filed on and after December 12, 1980. The maintenance fee must be paid at the stipulated times to maintain the patent in force. After the patent has expired anyone may make, use, or sell the invention without permission of the patentee, provided that matter covered by other unexpired patents is not used. The terms may not be extended except by special act of Congress except for certain pharmaceuticals.

Chapter 23: Maintenance Fees

All utility patents which issue from applications filed on and after December 12, 1980 are subject to the payment of maintenance fees which must be paid to maintain the patent in force. These fees are due at 3 1/2, 7 1/2 and 11 1/2 years from the date the patent is granted and can be paid without a surcharge during the "window-period" which is the six month period preceding each due date, e.g., 3 years to 3 years and six months, etc. See fee schedule for a list of maintenance fees.

Failure to pay the current maintenance fee on time may result in expiration of the patent. A six month grace period is provided when the maintenance fee may be paid with a surcharge. The grace period is the six month period immediately following the due date. The Patent and Trademark Office does not mail notices to patent owners that maintenance fees are due. If, however, the maintenance fee is not paid on time, efforts are made to remind the responsible party that the maintenance fee may be paid during the grace period with a surcharge.

Patents relating to some pharmaceutical inventions may be extended by the Commissioner for up to five years to compensate for marketing delays due to Federal pre-marketing regulatory procedures. Patents relating to all other types of inventions can only be extended by enactment of special Federal legislation.

Chapter 24: Correction Of Patents

Once the patent is granted, it is outside the jurisdiction of the Patent and Trademark Office except in a few respects. The Office may issue without charge a certificate correcting a clerical error it has made in the patent when the printed patent does not correspond to the record in the Office. These are mostly corrections of typographical errors made in printing. Some minor errors of a typographical nature made by the applicant may be corrected by a certificate of correction for which a charge is made.

The patentee may disclaim one or more claims of this patent by filing in the Office a disclaimer as provided by the statute. When the patent is defective in certain respects, the law provides that the patentee may apply for a reissue patent. This is a patent granted to replace the original and is granted only for the balance of the unexpired term. However, the nature of the changes that can be made by means of the reissue are rather limited; new matter cannot be added.

Any person may file a request for reexamination of a patent, along with the required fee, on the basis of prior art consisting of patents or printed publications. At the conclusion of the reexamination proceedings, a certificate setting forth the results of the reexamination proceeding is issued.

Chapter 25: Assignments And Licenses

A patent is personal property and may be sold to others or mortgaged; it may be bequeathed by a will, and it may pass to the heirs of deceased patentee. The patent law provides for the transfer or sale of a patent, or of an application for patent, by an instrument in writing. Such an instrument is referred to as an assignment and may transfer the entire interest in the patent.

The assignee, when the patent is assigned to him or her, becomes the owner of the patent and has the same rights that the original patentee had. The statute also provides for the assignment of a part interest, that is, a half interest, a fourth interest, etc., in a patent. There may also be a grant which conveys the same character of interest as an assignment but only for a particularly specified part of the United States.

A mortgage of patent property passes ownership thereof to the mortgagee or lender until the mortgage has been satisfied and a retransfer from the mortgagee back to the mortgagor, the borrower, is made. A conditional assignment also passes ownership of the patent and is regarded as absolute until canceled by the parties or by the decree of a competent court.

An assignment, grant, or conveyance of any patent or application for patent should be acknowledged before a notary public or officer authorized to administer oaths or perform notarial acts. The certificate of such acknowledgment constitutes prima facie evidence of the execution of the assignment, grant, or conveyance.

Recording of Assignments

The Office records assignments, grants, and similar instruments sent to it for recording, and the recording serves as notice. If an assignment, grant, or conveyance of a patent or an interest in a patent (or an application for patent) is not recorded in the Office within three months from its date, it is void against a subsequent purchaser for a valuable consideration without notice, unless it is recorded prior to the subsequent purchase.

An instrument relating to a patent should identify the patent by number and date (the name of the inventor and title of the invention as stated in the patent should also be given). An instrument relating to an application should identify the application by its serial number and date of filing, and the name of the inventor and title of the invention as stated in the application should also be given. Sometimes an assignment of an application is executed at the same time that the application is prepared and before it has been filed in the Office. Such assignment should adequately identify the application, as by its date of execution and name of the inventor and title of the invention, so that there can be no mistake as to the application intended.

If an application has been assigned and the assignment is recorded, on or before the date the issue fee is paid, the patent will be issued to the assignee as owner. If the assignment is of a part interest only, the patent will be issued to the inventor and assignee as joint owners.

Joint Ownership

Patents may be owned jointly by two or more persons as in the case of a patent granted to joint inventors, or in the case of the assignment of a part interest in a patent. Any joint owner of a patent, no matter how small the part interest, may make, use, and sell the invention for his or her own profit, without regard to the other owner, and may sell the interest or any part of it, or grant licenses to others, without regard to the other joint owner, unless the joint owners have made a contract governing their relation to each other. It is accordingly dangerous to assign a part interest without a definite agreement between the parties as to the extent of their respective rights and their obligations to each other if the above result is to be avoided.

The owner of a patent may grant licenses to others. Since the patentee has the right to exclude others from making, using or selling the invention, no one else may do any of these things without his permission. A license is the permission granted by the patent owner to another to make, use, or sell the invention. No particular form of license is required; a license is a contract and may include whatever provisions the parties agree upon, including the payment of royalties, etc.

The drawing up of a license agreement (as well as assignments) is within the field of an attorney at law, although such attorney should be familiar with patent matters as well. A few States have prescribed certain formalities to be observed in connection with the sale of patent rights.

Chapter 26: Patent Marking And Patent Pending

When an applicant who has filed for the patent but has not been granted patent i.e. his patent application is under consideration then the term patent pending applies. Patent pending enables an applicant to prevent their invention from being used by others. So they can use the term patent applied for etc to warn others from using their invention for their own purpose.

However, there are also rules which warn those who try to marks any product or procedure as patent pending; different countries adopt different policies so far as patent pending requests are concerned. To patent a product one has to submit an application in the patent office; upon verification the application is either accepted or rejected. In the application the applicant provides detail about his invention and makes claim that he should be given patent of the product or concept which he has invented.

Generally, the application is filed in the patent office which falls under the jurisdiction of the applicant which in majority of the cases is the country in which the applicant is residing. However there are regional forums also like European Patent Office where also the application can be filed.

There are several cases wherein during the patent period someone tries to use the concept of the patentee for business purpose or for some other purpose. This is termed as patent infringement. Patent infringement means others trying to use a patentee's technique for making profit or for his personal motive without taking the consent of the patentee. It is illegal and the patentee has all the rights to take legal action against those persons or organization.

A patentee who makes or sells patented articles or a person who does so for or under the patentee is required to mark the articles with the word "Patent" and the number of the patent. The penalty for failure to mark is that the patentee may not recover damages from an infringer unless the infringer was duly notified of the infringement and continued to infringe after the notice.

The marking of an article as patented when it is not in fact patented is against the law and subjects the offender to a penalty.

Some persons mark articles sold with the terms "Patent Applied For" or "Patent Pending." These phrases have no legal effect, but only give information that an application for patent has been filed in the Patent and Trademark Office. The protection afforded by a patent does not start until the actual grant of the patent. False use of these phrases or their equivalent is prohibited.

Design Patents

The patent laws provide for the granting of design patents to any person who has invented any new, original and ornamental design for an article of manufacture. The design patent protects only the appearance of an article, and not its structure or utilitarian features. The proceedings relating to granting of design patents are the same as those relating to other patents with a few differences.

See current fee schedule for the filing fee for a design application. A design patent has a term of 14 years, and no fees are necessary to maintain a design patent in force. If on examination it is determined that an applicant is entitled to a design patent under the law, a notice of allowance will be sent to the applicant or applicant's attorney, or agent, calling for the payment of an issue fee.

The drawing of the design patent conforms to the same rules as other drawings, but no reference characters are required.

The specification of a design application is short and ordinarily follows a set form. Only one claim is permitted, following a set form.

Plant Patents

The law also provides for the granting of a patent to anyone who has invented or discovered and asexually reproduced any distinct and new variety of plant, including cultivated sports, mutants, hybrids, and newly found seedlings, other than a tuber propagated plant or a plant found in an uncultivated state.

Asexually propagated plants are those that are reproduced by means other than from seeds, such as by the rooting of cuttings, by layering, budding, grafting, inarching, etc. With reference to tuber-propagated plants, for which a plant patent cannot be obtained, the term "tuber" is used in its narrow horticultural sense as meaning a short, thickened portion of an underground branch. The only plants covered by the term "tuber propagated" are the Irish potato and the Jerusalem artichoke.

An application for a plant patent consists of the same parts as other applications. A plant patent has term of 17 years. The application papers for a plant patent and any responsive papers pursuant to the prosecution must be filed in duplicate but only one need be signed (in the case of the application papers the original should be signed); the second copy may be a legible copy of the original. The reason for providing an original and duplicate file is that the duplicate file is sent to the Agricultural Research Service, Department of Agriculture for an advisory report on the plant variety.

The specification should include a complete detailed description of the plant and the characteristics thereof that distinguish the same over related known varieties, and its antecedents, expressed in botanical terms in the general form followed in standard botanical text books or publications dealing with the varieties of the kind of plant involved (evergreen tree, dahlia plant, rose plant, apple tree, etc.), rather than a mere broad non-botanical characterization such as commonly found in nursery or seed catalogs. The specification should also include the origin or parentage of the plant variety sought to be patented and must particularly point out where and in what manner the variety of plant has been asexually reproduced. Where colour is a distinctive feature of the plant the colour should be positively identified in the specification by reference to a designated colour as given by a recognized colour dictionary. Where the plant variety originated as a newly found seedling, the specification must fully describe the conditions (cultivation, environment, etc.) under which the seedling was found growing to establish that it was not found in an uncultivated state. A plant patent is granted on the entire plant. It therefore follows that only one claim is necessary and only one is permitted.

The oath or declaration required of the applicant in addition to the statements required for other applications must include the statement that the applicant has asexually reproduced the new plant variety.

Plant patent drawings are not mechanical drawings and should be artistically and competently executed. The drawing must disclose all the distinctive characteristics of the plant capable of visual representation. When colour is a distinguishing characteristic of the new variety, the drawing must be in colour. Two duplicate copies of colour drawings must be submitted. Colour drawings may be made either in permanent water colour or oil or in lieu thereof may be photographs made by colour photography or properly coloured on sensitized paper. The paper in any case must correspond in size, weight, and quality to the paper required for other drawings. Mounted photographs are acceptable.

Specimens of the plant variety, its flower or fruit, should not be submitted unless specifically called for by the examiner. The filing fee on each plant application and the issue fee can be found in the fee schedule. For a qualifying small entity filing and issue fees are reduced by half. All inquiries relating to plant patents and pending plant patent applications should be directed to the Patent and Trademark Office and not to the Department of Agriculture.

The Plant Variety Protection Act (Public Law 91-577), approved December 24, 1970) provides for a system of protection for sexually reproduced varieties, for which protection was not previously provided, under the administration of a Plant Variety Protection Office within the Department of Agriculture. Requests for information regarding the protection of sexually reproduced varieties should be addressed to Commissioner, Plant Variety Protection Office, Agricultural Marketing Service, National Agricultural Library Bldg., Room 500, 10301 Baltimore Blvd., Beltsville, Md. 20705-2351

Chapter 27: Infringement Of Patents

Patent provides an organization or individual exclusive rights to protect their products or concepts from the others. For a specified period of time the patent rights are provided to the individual and during those specified period the patentee is free to use his concept for doing business or for any personal purposes.

However, if anyone tries to use the patentees" concept, product or technique to make profits then this is termed a patent infringement. If an individual is protected by means of a patent infringement insurance plan, then it would prove to be most helpful in such situations.

Patent infringement means others trying to use a patentee's technique for making profit or for his personal motive without taking the consent of the patentee. It is illegal and the patentee has all the rights to take legal action against those persons or organization.

There are two type infringement direct infringement and indirect infringement. In case of direct someone directly tries to copy the techniques of the patentee while in case of indirect a third party who is the supplier of the product is involved.

Patent infringement insurance is available in some counties like United State and Western Europe. If you have patent insurance, the insurance company will takes the responsibility of providing economical help to the patentee in case he has to suffer any loses. Nowadays the term patent pirates are also being used in place of patent infringement.

Infringement of a patent consists in the unauthorized making, using, or selling of the patented invention within the territory of the United States, during the term of the patent. If a patent is infringed, the patentee may sue for relief in the appropriate Federal court. The patentee may ask the court for an injunction to prevent the continuation of the infringement and may also ask the court for an award of damages because of the infringement. In such an infringement suit, the defendant may raise the question of the validity of the patent, which is then decided by the court.

The defendant may also aver that what is being done does not constitute infringement. Infringement is determined primarily by the language of the claims of the patent and, if what the defendant is making does not fall within the language of any of the claims of the patent, there is no infringement.

Suits for infringement of patents follow the rules of procedure of the Federal courts. From the decision of the district court, there is an appeal to the Court of Appeals for the Federal Circuit. The Supreme Court may thereafter take a case by writ of certiorari. If the United States Government infringes a patent, the patentee has a remedy for damages in the United States Claims Court. The Government may use any patented invention without permission of the patentee, but the patentee is entitled to obtain compensation for the use by or for the Government.

If the patentee notifies anyone that is infringing the patent or threatens suit, the one charged with infringement may start the suit in a Federal court.

The Office has no jurisdiction over questions relating to infringement of patents. In examining applications for patent, no determination is made as to whether the invention sought to be patented infringes any prior patent. An improvement invention may be patentable, but it might infringe a prior unexpired patent for the invention improved upon, if there is one.

Chapter 28: Treaties And Foreign Patents

Since the rights granted by a United States patent extend only throughout the territory of the United States and have no effect in a foreign country, an inventor who wishes patent protection in other countries must apply for a patent in each of the other countries or in regional patent offices. Almost every country has its own patent law, and a person desiring a patent in a particular country must make an application for patent in that country, in accordance with the requirements of that country.

The laws of many countries differ in various respects from the patent law of the United States. In most foreign countries, publication of the invention before the date of the application will bar the right to a patent. In most foreign countries maintenance fees are required. Most foreign countries require that the patented invention must be manufactured in that country after a certain period, usually three years. If there is no manufacture within this period, the patent may be void in some countries, although in most countries the patent may be subject to the grant of compulsory licenses to any person who may apply for a license.

There is a treaty relating to patents which is adhered to by 100 countries, including the United States, and is known as the Paris Convention for the Protection of Industrial Property. It provides that each country guarantees to the citizens of the other countries the same rights in patent and trademark matters that it gives to its own citizens.

The treaty also provides for the right of priority in the case of patents, trademarks and industrial designs (design patents). This right means that, on the basis of a regular first application filed in one of the member countries, the applicant may, within a certain period of time, apply for protection in all the other member countries.

These later applications will then be regarded as if they had been filed on the same day as the first application. Thus, these later applicants will have priority over applications for the same invention which may have been filed during the same period of time by other persons. Moreover, these later applications, being based on the first application, will not be invalidated by any acts accomplished in the interval, such as, for example, publication or exploitation of the invention, the sale of copies of the design, or use of the trademark. The period of time mentioned above, within which the subsequent applications may be filed in the other countries, is 12 months in the case of first applications for patent and six months in the case of industrial designs and trademarks.

Another treaty, known as the Patent Cooperation Treaty, was negotiated at a diplomatic conference in Washington, D. C. in June of 1970. The treaty came into force on January 24, 1978, and is presently adhered to by 44 countries, including the United States. The treaty facilitates the filing of applications for patent on the same invention in member countries by providing, among other things, for centralized filing procedures and a standardized application format.

The timely filing of an international application affords applicants an international filing date in each country which is designated in the international application and provides:
(1) A search of the invention and
(2) A later time period within which the national applications for patent must be filed.

A number of patent attorneys specialize in obtaining patents in foreign countries. In general, an inventor should be satisfied that he could make some profit from foreign patents or that there is some particular reason for obtaining them, before he attempts to apply for foreign patents.

Under United States law it is necessary, in the case of inventions made in the United States, to obtain a license from the Commissioner of Patents and Trademarks before applying for a patent in a foreign country. Such a license is required if the foreign application is to be filed before an application is filed in the United States or before the expiration of six months from the filing of an application in the United States. The filing of an application for patent constitutes the request for a license and the granting or denial of such request is indicated in the filing receipt mailed to each applicant. After six months from the United States filing, a license is not required unless the invention has been ordered to be kept secret. If the invention has been ordered to be kept secret, the consent to the filing abroad must be obtained from the Commissioner of Patents and Trademarks during the period the order of secrecy is in effect.

Chapter 29: Foreign Applicants For United State Patents

The patent laws of the United States make no discrimination with respect to the citizenship of the inventor. Any inventor, regardless of his citizenship, may apply for a patent on the same basis as a U.S. citizen. There are, however, a number of particular points of special interest to applicants located in foreign countries.

The application for patent in the United States must be made by the inventor and the inventor must sign the oath or declaration (with certain exceptions), differing from the law in many countries where the signature of the inventor and an oath of inventorship are not necessary. If the inventor is dead, the application may be made by his executor or administrator, or equivalent, and in the case of mental disability it may be made by his legal representative (guardian).

No United States patent can be obtained if the invention was patented abroad before applying in the United States by the inventor or his legal representatives or assigns on an application filed more than 12 months before filing in the United States. Six months are allowed in the case of a design patent.

An application for a patent filed in the United States by any person who has previously regularly filed an application for a patent for the same invention in a foreign country which affords similar privileges to citizens of the United States shall have the same force and effect for the purpose of overcoming intervening acts of others as if filed in the

United States on the date on which the application for a patent for the same invention was first filed in such foreign country, provided the application in the United States is filed within 12 months (six months in the case of a design patent) from the earliest date on which any such foreign application was filed. A copy of the foreign application certified by the patent office of the country in which it was filed is required to secure this right of priority.

If any application for patent has been filed in any foreign country by the applicant or by his legal representatives or assigns prior to his application in the United States, the applicant must, in the oath or declaration accompanying the application, state the country in which the earliest such application has been filed, giving the date of filing the application; and all applications filed more than a year before the filing in the United States must also be recited in the oath or declaration.

An oath or declaration must be made with respect to every application. When the applicant is in a foreign country the oath or affirmation may be before any diplomatic or consular officer of the United States, or before any officer having an official seal and authorized to administer oaths in the foreign country, whose authority shall be proved by a certificate of a diplomatic or consular officer of the United States, the oath being attested in all cases by the proper official seal of the officer before whom the oath is made.

When the oath is taken before an officer in the country foreign to the United States, all the application papers (except the drawing) must be attached together and a ribbon passed one or more times through all the sheets of the application, and the ends of the ribbons brought together under the seal before the latter is affixed and impressed, or each sheet must be impressed with the official seal of the officer before whom the oath was taken. If the application is filed by the legal representative (executive, administrator, etc.) of a deceased inventor, the legal representative must make the oath or declaration.

When a declaration is used, the ribboning procedure is not necessary, nor is it necessary to appear before an official in connection with the making of a declaration.

A foreign applicant may be represented by any patent attorney or agent who is registered to practice before the United States Patent and Trademark Office.

Chapter 30: Fees And Payment

A patent protects your valuable invention from unauthorized usage. Just imagine you doing all the hard work and someone else taking the credit. You can avoid such a situation by applying for a patent. Once you obtain a patent no one can steal or copy your patent. A patent is nothing but a set of rights that are given by the government in order to protect your invention from any unauthorized usage. A person who disobeys the patent laws is likely to go to jail.

If you have entrusted the responsibility of acquiring a patent to a lawyer then the cost for getting a patent is high. Cost for getting a patent is comparatively less if you decide to acquire a patent on your own. You should have sufficient knowledge about patent laws if you decide to get a patent on your own. If you want to keep the costs down then you should have a thorough knowledge about how to get a patent.

If you don't have any knowledge about the cost for getting a patent then you can always refer the internet. Cost for getting a patent in the European countries is more as compared to cost of getting a patent in United States.

Estimating the cost for getting a patent depend on the invention you have invented. It also depends on the technology that is used in the invention. The fee structure in most countries for getting a patent has changed.

Below are fees for filing patent In United

(a) General Fees:
(1) FILING AND BASIC NATIONAL FEES. -

(A) On filing each application for an original patent, except for design, plant, or provisional applications, $300.

(B) On filing each application for an original design patent, $200.

(C) On filing each application for an original plant patent, $200.

(D) On filing each provisional application for an original patent, $200.

(E) On filing each application for the reissue of a patent, $300.

(F) The basic national fee for each international application filed under the treaty defined in section 351(a) of this title entering the national stage under section 371 of this title, $300.

(G) In addition, excluding any sequence listing or computer program listing filed in electronic medium as prescribed by the Director, for any application the specification and drawings of which exceed 100 sheets of paper (or equivalent as prescribed by the Director if filed in an electronic medium), $250 for each additional 50 sheets of paper (or equivalent as prescribed by the Director if filed in an electronic medium) or fraction thereof.

(2) EXCESS CLAIMS FEES. - In addition to filing and basic national fees.

(A) On filing or on presentation at any other time, $200 for each claim in independent form in excess of 3;

(B) On filing or on presentation at any other time, $50 for each claim (whether dependent or independent) in excess of 20; and

(C) For each application containing a multiple dependent claim, $360.

For the purpose of computing fees under this paragraph, a multiple dependent claim referred to in section 112 of this title or any claim depending there from shall be considered as separate dependent claims in accordance with the number of claims to which reference is made. The Director may by regulation provide for a refund of any part of the fee specified in this paragraph for any claim that is canceled before an examination on the merits, as prescribed by the Director, has been made of the application under section 131 of this title. Errors in payment of the additional fees under this paragraph may be rectified in accordance with regulations prescribed by the Director.

(3) EXAMINATION FEES. -

(A) For examination of each application for an original patent, except for design, plant, provisional, or international applications, $200.

(B) For examination of each application for an original design patent, $130.

(C) For examination of each application for an original plant patent, $160.

(D) For examination of the national stage of each international application, $200.

(E) For examination of each application for the reissue of a patent, $600.

The provisions of section 111(a) of this title relating to the payment of the fee for filing the application shall apply to the payment of the fee specified in this paragraph with respect to an application filed under section 111(a) of this title. The provisions of section 371(d) of this title relating to the payment of the national fee shall apply to the payment of the fee specified in this paragraph with respect to an international application.

(4) ISSUE FEES. -

(A) For issuing each original patent, except for design or plant patents, $1,400.

(B) For issuing each original design patent, $800.

(C) For issuing each original plant patent, $1,100.

(D) For issuing each reissue patent, $1,400.
(5) DISCLAIMER FEE. - On filing each disclaimer, $130.

(6) APPEAL FEES. -

(A) On filing an appeal from the examiner to the Board of Patent Appeals and Interferences, $500.

(B) In addition, on filing a brief in support of the appeal, $500, and on requesting an oral hearing in the appeal before the Board of Patent Appeals and Interferences, $1,000.

(7) REVIVAL FEES. - On filing each petition for the revival of an unintentionally abandoned application for a patent, for the unintentionally delayed payment of the fee for issuing each patent, or for an unintentionally delayed response by the patent owner in any reexamination proceeding, $1,500, unless the petition is filed under section 133 or 151 of this title, in which case the fee shall be $500.

(8) EXTENSION FEES. - For petitions for 1-month extensions of time to take actions required by the Director in an application -

(A) On filing a first petition, $120;

(B) On filing a second petition, $330; and

(C) On filing a third or subsequent petition, $570.

(b) MAINTENANCE FEES. - The Director shall charge the following fees for maintaining in force all patents based on applications filed on or after December 12, 1980:

(1) 3 years and 6 months after grant, $900.

(2) 7 years and 6 months after grant, $2,300.

(3) 11 years and 6 months after grant, $3,800.

Unless payment of the applicable maintenance fee is received in the United States Patent and Trademark Office on or before the date the fee is due or within a grace period of 6 months thereafter, the patent will expire as of the end of such grace period. The Director may require the payment of a surcharge as a condition of accepting within such 6-month grace period the payment of an applicable maintenance fee. No fee may be established for maintaining a design or plant patent in force.

(Dec. 8, 2004, Public Law 108-447, sec. 801, 118 Stat. 2809.)

The bracketed text below is the unamended text of 35 U.S.C. 41(a) and (b), which may continue to have effect following fiscal year 2006:

[(a) The Director shall charge the following fees:

(1)
(A) On filing each application for an original patent, except in design or plant cases, $690.

(B) In addition, on filing or on presentation at any other time, $78 for each claim in independent form which is in excess of 3, $18 for each claim (whether independent or dependent) which is in excess of 20, and $260 for each application containing a multiple dependent claim.

(C) On filing each provisional application for an original patent, $150.

(2) For issuing each original or reissue patent, except in design or plant cases, $1,210.

(3) In design and plant cases-
(A) On filing each design application, $310;

(B) On filing each plant application, $480;

(C) On issuing each design patent, $430; and

(D) On issuing each plant patent, $580.

(4)
(A) On filing each application for the reissue of a patent, $690.

(B) In addition, on filing or on presentation at any other time, $78 for each claim in independent form which is in excess of the number of independent claims of the original patent, and

$18 for each claim (whether independent or dependent) which is in excess of 20 and also in excess of the number of claims of the original patent.

(5) On filing each disclaimer, $110.

(6)
(A) On filing an appeal from the examiner to the Board of Patent Appeals and Interferences, $300.

(B) In addition, on filing a brief in support of the appeal, $300, and on requesting an oral hearing in the appeal before the Board of Patent Appeals and Interferences, $260.

(7)
On filing each petition for the revival of an unintentionally abandoned application for a patent, for the unintentionally delayed payment of the fee for issuing each patent, or for an unintentionally delayed response by the patent owner in any reexamination proceeding, $1,210, unless the petition is filed under section 133 or 151 of this title, in which case the fee shall be $110.

(8)
For petitions for 1-month extensions of time to take actions required by the Director in an application-

(A) On filing a first petition, $110;

(B) On filing a second petition, $270; and

(C) On filing a third or subsequent petition, $490.

(9)
Basic national fee for an international application where the Patent and Trademark Office was the International Preliminary Examining Authority and the International Searching Authority, $670.

(10)
Basic national fee for an international application where the Patent and Trademark Office was the International Searching Authority but not the International Preliminary Examining Authority, $690.

(11)
Basic national fee for an international application where the Patent and Trademark Office was neither the International Searching Authority nor the International Preliminary Examining Authority, $970.

(12)
Basic national fee for an international application where the international preliminary examination has been paid to the Patent and Trademark Office, and the international preliminary examination report states that the provisions of Article 33 (2), (3), and (4) of the Patent Cooperation Treaty have been satisfied for all claims in the application entering the national stage, $96.

(13)

For filing or later presentation of each independent claim in the national stage of an international application in excess of 3, $78.

(14)

For filing or later presentation of each claim (whether independent or dependent) in a national stage of an international application in excess of 20, $18.

(15)

For each national stage of an international application containing a multiple dependent claim, $260. For the purpose of computing fees, a multiple dependent claim as referred to in section 112 of this title or any claim depending there from shall be considered as separate dependent claims in accordance with the number of claims to which reference is made. Errors in payment of the additional fees may be rectified in accordance with regulations of the Director.

(b) The Director shall charge the following fees for maintaining in force all patents based on applications filed on or after December 12, 1980:

(1) 3 years and 6 months after grant, $830.

(2) 7 years and 6 months after grant, $1,900.

(3) 11 years and 6 months after grant, $2,910. Unless payment of the applicable maintenance fee is received in the Patent and Trademark Office on or before the date the

fee is due or within a grace period of six months thereafter, the patent will expire as of the end of such grace period. The Director may require the payment of a surcharge as a condition of accepting within such 6-month grace period the payment of an applicable maintenance fee. No fee may be established for maintaining a design or plant patent in force.]

(c)
(1) The Director may accept the payment of any maintenance fee required by subsection (b) of this section which is made within twenty-four months after the six-month grace period if the delay is shown to the satisfaction of the Director to have been unintentional, or at any time after the six-month grace period if the delay is shown to the satisfaction of the Director to have been unavoidable. The Director may require the payment of a surcharge as a condition of accepting payment of any maintenance fee after the six-month grace period. If the Director accepts payment of a maintenance fee after the six-month grace period, the patent shall be considered as not having expired at the end of the grace period.

(2) A patent, the term of which has been maintained as a result of the acceptance of a payment of a maintenance fee under this subsection, shall not abridge or affect the right of any person or that person's successors in business who made, purchased, offered to sell, or used anything protected by the patent within the United States, or imported anything protected by the patent into the United States after the 6-month grace period but prior to the acceptance of a maintenance fee under this subsection, to continue the use

of, to offer for sale, or to sell to others to be used, offered for sale, or sold, the specific thing so made, purchased, offered for sale, used, or imported. The court before which such matter is in question may provide for the continued manufacture, use, offer for sale, or sale of the thing made, purchased, offered for sale, or used within the United States, or imported into the United States, as specified, or for the manufacture, use, offer for sale, or sale in the United States of which substantial preparation was made after the 6-month grace period but before the acceptance of a maintenance fee under this subsection, and the court may also provide for the continued practice of any process that is practiced, or for the practice of which substantial preparation was made, after the 6-month grace period but before the acceptance of a maintenance fee under this subsection, to the extent and under such terms as the court deems equitable for the protection of investments made or business commenced after the 6-month grace period but before the acceptance of a maintenance fee under this subsection.

THE ABOVE PRICES ARE SUBJECT TO CHANGE WITHOUT NOTICE.

All payment of money required for Patent and Trademark Office fees should be made in United States specie, Treasury notes, national bank notes, post office money orders or postal notes payable to the Commissioner of Patents and Trademarks, or by certified checks. If sent in any other form, the Office may delay or cancel the credit until collection is made. Postage stamps are not acceptable. Money orders and checks must be made payable to the

Commissioner of Patents and Trademarks. Remittances from foreign countries must be payable and immediately negotiable in the United States for the full amount of the fee required. Money paid by actual mistake or in excess, such as a payment not required by law, will be refunded, but a mere change of purpose after the payment of money, as when a party desires to withdraw his application for a patent or to withdraw an appeal, will not entitle a party to demand such a return. Amounts of $1.00 or less will not be returned unless specifically demanded, within a reasonable time.

Chapter 31: Conclusion

Today, many people tend to be confused on what copyright, patent and trademark is all about. Many people tend to neglect the importance of these things. First of all, when you start your own business, you should have a trademark for your business. A trademark is a kind of symbol or logo that you put in your products to distinguish it from other products made by other companies. For example, if you are in the apparel business, you should have a unique trademark for your clothes, shoes and pants. By having your own trademark, you can be sure that your clients will know what they are buying.

If you made a new building design, or if you composed a song or poet, you have to copyright it in order to prevent it from being used without your permission. By copyrighting your songs, your architectural designs, or your documents, you can be sure that it will make it illegal to be used by other people without your permission. It is important that you should copyright your documents in order to prevent others from profiting from it. For example, if you composed a new song and were a hit with the public and you didn't copyright it, you will see that someone else will claim that they wrote the song and will prevent you from using the song without their permission.

The same thing goes in patenting an invention. By patenting a particular invention, you can make sure that you will have absolute right for it and claim it as yours where no one will be authorized to copy it. Patenting, copyrighting and trademarks are all in the intellectual property law. You have to consider that this law is made to provide protection on intellectual property and is a special branch of the law that requires a special kind of lawyer.

Trademark registration, patenting, and copyrighting are all handled by the United States Patent and Trademark Office or PTO. The PTO is responsible for patenting all kinds of inventions and they are also responsible for registering trademarks and copyrighting.

If you recently invented a new kind of gadget which is original and fully functional on its purpose, you can apply for a patent. By patenting your invention, you can be sure that no one else will be able to claim the invention as theirs. However, you have to consider that patenting an invention will take a lot of time and will cost a lot of money. This is why you should be financially prepared for it. You should also consider the fact that you will need a patent and trademark lawyer for it to represent you during the entire process of patenting your invention.

You have to consider that the patenting process is a complex process which deals with the intellectual property law. You will also need a lot of requirements for it, such as a prototype of your invention that you need to demonstrate with the PTO. The PTO will determine whether it can be approved or rejected of patenting.

In the trademark registration process, you have to present your trademark symbol to the PTO. Although the process for trademark registration is shorter than patenting an invention, you have to consider that it will also take some time. You will need to present a minimum requirement, such as a trademark design and your business registration. Once you have the minimum requirements needed to file for trademark registration, the next step is by letting a PTO lawyer examine the trademark and determine whether it bears a resemblance with other kinds of trademarks that is already registered.

There are specific grounds for approval and refusal of trademark where the PTO lawyer will base their decisions. If your trademark symbol contains a lot of similarities with other trademark symbol that is already registered, it will usually be refused.

These are the basics in patent, copyright and trademarks. As you can see, it is very important to get your inventions, your architectural designs and trademark logo registered with the PTO to protect it from being used without your permission or get it stolen and be claimed by other people.

So, the next time you successfully invented something or you have a new business trademark symbol, or if you wrote a new song or designed a new building, get it patented, copyrighted or registered in the PTO immediately.

Acquiring a patent for your invention is like protecting your patent from any form of malpractices. Exclusive rights are given to the inventor that help to protect the invention.

These exclusive rights are granted for a limited period. However to get a patent for your invention it must be inventive, new and useful. Every country has its own methods and criteria for issuing patents.

You cannot get a patent unless your invention is something constructive. It must also be new. A mere idea or a suggestion cannot give you a patent. Methods of doing printed matter or business cannot be patented. A person desiring a patent for his or her invention should be confident that the invention will be useful for others. Many inventors after getting a patent ask the question that how long does a patent last.

How long does a patent last will depend on the type of patent. A patent can either be a utility patent or a design patent. Utility patents are given more time duration than design patent. Utility patents protect any new functional improvements or invention on existing inventions.

The existing invention can be a composition, machine, product or even a process. For example if you want to invent a better carburetor or a new recipe then you would require a utility patent. Generally utility patents are given a duration of 20 years. In case of utility patents the duration is calculated from the day you file the patent application.

14 years are granted for design patent. In case of design patents the duration is calculated from the day your patent is granted. Design patent protect the configuration, ornamental design, shape or form of an invention or improved decorative appearance. If you want to change an existing product in style then you will have to apply for a design patent.

Duration can be extended under exceptional situations. After the duration of the patent expires, the person who owns the inventions loses the right of excluding others from utilizing his or her invention. That means anyone can now use the invention without taking any permission from the patent holder. It is a must to get a patent for an invention to protect it from malicious intentions.

But if anyone tries to use the invention before the patent expires, then the patent holder can take legal action against that person. During this period copying any form such as photocopy, electronic, mechanical is strictly prohibited. Any other person also cannot sell or import the invention. Patents have played a very important role in curbing such mal practices.

Typically patent owners can seek monetary compensation to those who violate patent laws before the patent expiry period. Once the patent period becomes invalid, you cannot simply do anything against these infringers.

In most countries, individuals as well as corporate companies are granted patents.

The following websites were referenced in researching this book:

http://www.aaglobalsourcing.com/

http://www.qualitywebdesign.aaglobalsourcing.com/

http://www.findapropertyuk.aaglobalsourcing.com/

http://www.improvenetprofit.aaglobalsourcing.com/

http://www.nutritionforsportandexercise.aaglobalsourcing.com/

http://www.quickweightlossproducts.aaglobalsourcing.com/

http://www.howtowhitenteethathome.aaglobalsourcing.com/

http://www.pethealthsolutions.aaglobalsourcing.com/

http://www.sexualenhancers.aaglobalsourcing.com/

http://www.onlinefashionshopping.aaglobalsourcing.com/

http://www.marketplace.aaglobalsourcing.com/

http://www.vacancy2.aaglobalsourcing.com/

http://www.cheapesthealthinsurance.aaglobalsourcing.com/

http://www.ifa.aaglobalsourcing.com/

http://www.financialadviser.aaglobalsourcing.com/

http://www.forextradingsystem.aaglobalsourcing.com/

http://www.onlineforextrading.aaglobalsourcing.com/

http://www.aetnahealthinsurance.aaglobalsourcing.com/

http://www.familyhealthinsurance.aaglobalsourcing.com/

http://www.bpo.aaglobalsourcing.com/

http://www.booksonline.aaglobalsourcing.com/

http://www.bestpensionprovider.aaglobalsourcing.com/

http://www.mortgageforpeoplewithbadcredit.aaglobalsourcing.com/

http://www.mutualfundsinvestment.aaglobalsourcing.com/

http://www.inheritancetaxes.aaglobalsourcing.com/

www.ingramcontent.com/pod-product-compliance
Lightning Source LLC
Chambersburg PA
CBHW051541170526
45165CB00002B/827